Kevin & Angie

I hope you
enjoy the book.

12-02-06

What others are saying about this book:

"You can't understand the game without a program. You can't win in the office without knowing the players. *Corporate Games* not only describes the players, it shows you how to handle them. Insightful, fascinating and fun. Highly recommended.
—Dan Poynter, author/publisher. http://ParaPub.com

"Finally a book that takes an honest look at today's corporate workplace. This book will make you laugh, think and help you to enjoy your job."
—R. Michael Allen, MD - Psychiatrist

"Interesting, fun approach to corporate culture."
—Jay Batista, VP Sales & Marketing, Harris Corporation

"*Corporate Games* is an excellent guide to uncover corporate personalities and their intent. This book not only helps novices(new hires)gain perspective of these personalities, but experienced (tenured) employees to relate to and have more of an in-depth understanding of these characters. Everyone will enjoy the stories and great illustrations. Highly recommended."
—Leonard Kowalewski - Business Manager

"This original and candid piece of work will keep you entertained page upon page. The dilemma of feeling paralyzed by difficult personalities is no longer. This is a great resource for years to come."
—David Molinaro CEO-Orion Ventures

"*Corporate Games* provides an insightful, truthful look into today's work environment. Honest, funny, original, and easy to read. The pictures are awesome."
—Kieran O'Brien – small business employee

"From the new hire to the seasoned professional, *Corporate Games* will help all!"
—Kriss Wittmann – Trainer & Development Coach

"A refreshing new perspective on the types of people you'll encounter in today's business environment. Make this your guide to a healthier work environment."
—Diane Polnow, Business Sales Manager

"The pictures and back sections gave me practical insight that will help me enjoy my job even more."
—John Schultz, Retail Sales Manager
McKesson Corporation

Corporate Games
Don't Get Caught in the Rally!

Alan Hirschfeld

Damon Zimmer

Illustrations by
Jose Pardo

First Edition

Cool River Publishing – Monument, Colorado

Corporate Games
Don't Get Caught in the Rally!

Alan Hirschfeld

Damon Zimmer

Illustrations by
Jose Pardo

Published by:
Cool River Publishing
590 Highway 105 #301
Monument, CO 80132-9125
http://www.coolriverpub.com

Copyright ©2002 by Alan Hirschfeld and Damon Zimmer
First Published February, 2003

Printed in the United States of America

Library of Congress Cataloging-in-Publication Data
Hirschfeld, Alan.
    Corporate games : don't get caught in the rally /
Alan Hirschfeld, Damon Zimmer ; illustrations by Jose
Pardo. — 1st ed.
        p. cm.
    Includes bibliographical references and index.
    LCCN 2002094415
    ISBN 0-9722566-0-1
    1. Office politics. 2. Psychology, Industrial.
3. Personality and occupation. 4. Interpersonal relations.
I. Zimmer, Damon. II. Title.

HF5386.5.H57 2003   650.1'3
                QBI02-200671

Contents

To Uncle Kemp

Thank you for your support and encouragement.

You will be dearly missed.

About the Authors

Alan Hirschfeld and Damon Zimmer bring over thirty combined years of everyday business experience to *Corporate Games*. They are committed to deliver the best performance possible on the job, and have firsthand experience with a wide variety of personalities in the workplace. Their passion to help people realize more success in life—on and off the job—is the driving force behind this, their first book.

Alan has twenty years of business experience with a gamut of companies ranging from Fortune 100 businesses to those with less than ten employees. His work experience includes sales, technical sales support, engineering, software development, project management, and marketing. Alan holds a Bachelors of Industrial Engineering degree from the Georgia Institute of Technology and lives with his family in Monument, Colorado.

In Damon's ten years of business experience ranging from midsize to Fortune 100 companies, his passion for sales has led him to exceed quotas and be ranked as a sales leader. He holds a Bachelors Degree in Business Administration from California State University, Northridge, and lives with his family in Colorado Springs, Colorado.

Preface
Note to the Reader

With more than thirty years of working and interacting in the corporate world, we have witnessed and experienced the gamut from prosperous times of growth and good fortune to the business downturn of recent times, which includes employee layoffs, cutbacks and bankruptcies.

Corporations today continue to fight for a competitive edge and survival. The focus on the bottom line has become their critical driving force. To maintain current momentum (or enhance market position) these companies expect their employees to be more productive with fewer resources. This could affect you in several ways:

- Higher expectations for job performance (sometimes for less pay),
- Impetuous deadlines to be met, and
- Additional projects with increased obstacles standing in your way of success.

Many of these obstacles include events and co-workers you can't control. One of the most significant roadblocks we hear about in today's workplace is, "How do I work with difficult people in the workplace?"

This book will provide you an insightful look into the many difficult personalities that exist in the ever-changing work environment, and leave you feeling empowered knowing you can work successfully with them. Employees working in Fortune 100 companies, small start-ups, or any company in between can relate to and apply the knowledge gained from this book. We developed insightful and creative stories along with original illustrations to bring the workplace to life. Each chapter will help you connect on both a visual and emotional level for a deeper understanding of its featured work personality. *Corporate Games* will also provide you with additional insight into the business world. It will offer you a creative way to successfully interact with many of these corporate personalities you presently encounter. Entry level, seasoned, and mature workers will find this book a great tool. It's your guidebook to understanding, identifying and interacting with these personalities; it helps you realize these personalities and their partners have a long-term effect on the workplace.

In addition, you will be able to apply what you have learned in this book to your work environment. You will know how to identify and avoid conflict with these personalities. You may recognize yourself in this book. You'll almost certainly recognize others.

The personality descriptions used in this book are examples of what you can encounter in the workplace. It should be noted the authors are not attempting to stereotype any of these personalities as to a particular build, age, sex, or national origin. The text, in conjunction with the illustrations, is merely our representations of what this personality could look like.

It has been said humor is food for the soul. We find a day at the office without humor is like going into the office early on a Monday and discovering the coffee machine is broken. Although a hot cup of "Joe" isn't necessary, it sure makes the day much more enjoyable. You may find our unique views in the book a bit outlandish, but we're confident it will make your reading more pleasurable and entertaining. Our avid movie viewing produced many quotes throughout this work to assist with the light-heartedness.

You may be curious about the cover subtitle *Don't Get Caught in the Rally*! There is a detailed explanation of this in the chapter *Let the Games be Understood*.

Our ultimate goal is to arm you with the knowledge and skill to deal with these personalities, be more successful in your career, and assist you in finding a way to enjoy your work. Knowledge is power, and this book provides you with just that.

Alan Hirschfeld – Monument, Colorado

Damon Zimmer – Colorado Springs, Colorado

Acknowledgements

Alan and Damon wish to acknowledge and thank the many people who provided support and inspiration along the way, including Steve Turre, Kristie A. Swanson, Staci Light, and Kari Sanders.

This book could not have been completed without the understanding of our wives and children. Thanks to Jennifer for her input, patience, understanding, support, and encouragement throughout the entire process. We wish to extend a special thanks to Sylvie for her patience, understanding, wonderful meals, hospitality, and great input—such as the *Gluteus Maximizer*. Thanks to Geoffrey for his concept contribution to the drawing *The Best of Breed*.

Thank you to all those who assisted with content edit, direction, and their time and commitment that provided valuable input to help in the development of this work. These include Nik B. Edes, Kieran O'Brien, Jay Batista, David Molinaro, Kriss Wittmann, R. Michael Allen, MD, Ian O'Brien, Leonard Kowalewski, Diane Polnow, and John Schultz.

We wish to extend a special thanks to Dan Poynter for his book *The Self Publishing Manual,* along with his direction in creating this work and the company Cool River Publishing. Thank you to friends and neighbors including Larry and Penny Dyer and Laurent Mbanda, Ph.D. for support, encouragement, and advice along the way.

Uncle Kemp started us off with our first funds, and we wish to extend a warm thank you and appreciation for his confidence and support to complete this work. Also, thanks to Michael Schiller for helping organize the publishing arm, Cool River Publishing, Inc. and to Peter Quittmeyer for his sound legal advice. Thank you to Jose Pardo, whose great vision and talent has led to the completed illustrations you see within this work and on the front cover. Thanks to all those who helped create this work including cover design (Robert Howard), content editor (Steve Wamberg), and copy edit and typesetting (Marty Shull).

We sincerely thank all of these fine people.

Lastly, we wish to extend a special thanks to God for the insight, inspiration and courage to finish this project.

Warning-Disclaimer

This book was written as a tool for education and entertainment. The authors are in no way implying any medical analysis or psychology in their descriptions and behavior of these characters. The content is purely observations and the authors' experiences in their thirty-plus combined years of working with, and in, corporations.

This book is sold with the understanding that the publisher, authors, and illustrator are not engaged in rendering any medical, legal, accounting or any other professional services. If medical, legal or other expert assistance is required, the services of a competent professional should be sought.

The intent of this book is to take a humorous and insightful look at several of the many personalities in the workplace. Some proposed solutions to identifying and interacting with these personalities, along with recognizing their partners and political alliances, are included in the book. Possible long-term effects upon you, other co-workers, and the employer are also explored.

Every effort has been made to make this book as complete and as accurate as possible. However, there may be mistakes, both typographical and in content. Therefore, this text should be used only as a general guide and not as the ultimate source of examining corporate personalities. Furthermore, this book contains information on corporate personalities that is current only up to the printing date.

Any character descriptions, stories, or illustrations that have any resemblance to any person, place or thing are purely coincidental. These stories were created to enhance this work and add humor.

The purpose of this book is to educate and entertain. The authors and Cool River Publishing shall have neither liability nor responsibility to any person or entity with respect to any loss or damage caused, or alleged to have been caused, directly or indirectly, by the information contained in this book.

What?
Do you got a problem with books?

No, I don't have a problem with books, but
why do you need 17 copies of it?

Well... in case I wanted to read it over
again.

My Blue Heaven

Let the Games be Understood

So you may be asking yourself, "How do I survive in today's corporate environment? How can I be more productive with my co-workers? Why do the people I'm working with seem to be playing games?"

Perhaps *avoiding* the game is your objective. We know it's nearly impossible to avoid all games in the workplace, and being caught up in one is miserable. Still, the key to working success is to gain a better understanding of those around you and how they operate in the work environment.

Though there are many frustrating personalities, you still must try and maintain successful working relationships. The most difficult working conditions occur when you are trying to be a productive employee around co-workers who seem to make your job more difficult than it needs to be. It's the corporate game they are playing. Many companies, large and small, have these games in play. You may not be aware or recognize these games, but they exist and are being rallied around you. We refer to these personalities as *Corporate Games Personalities*.

The book, **Corporate Games**, covers twenty-five *Corporate Games Personalities*, although we acknowledge there are many more. In this book you will encounter personalities such as the *Gluteus Maximizer* (smooching for a benefit), the *Napoleon* (the empire builder) and *Ascendo Inabilitus* (working at a level of incompetence). All of the personality names within this book originate from their respective dominant character trait. We intentionally kept them simple for easy identification and recollection. Many of your co-workers may possess the traits of some of these corporate personality types. You might, too.

Even though each of us demonstrates a dominant characteristic, it's common for an individual to be comprised of several personalities—we refer to them as a *Corporate Mutt*. Just like a dog that's composed of several breeds, this unique mongrel is a combination of several corporate personalities. These traits shape how an individual will interact in work situations and associate with co-workers and customers.

In **Corporate Games** we have created a fictitious company which we call Digitron. Digitron is an industry leader that manufactures and sells a wide variety of digits. This world-wide corporation has many plants and divisions.

Our purpose in creating Digitron for this book is to illustrate the complexity and inter-workings of today's corporations. The various divisions (manufacturing, field service, sales, and finance) are highlighted in stories within this work to communicate how the many diverse personalities in these departments interact with employees like you in the workplace. Digitron's exact Corporate structure, functionality, and products are intentionally left vague in order to focus on individual circumstances similar to what you will encounter in your work environment. Just as you are witnessing in the corporate world today, Digitron is engrossed in a tough economic climate.

There are twenty-five corporate personalities—each with their own chapter—highlighted in this work. Each one has a corresponding character drawing to help depict our perception of the respective *Corporate Games Personality*. These original pictures help capture the essence of our work. The goal is to help you better relate with the corporate players in your world. Make no mistake—you have, or probably will work with one or more of these corporate personalities at some point in your business career.

Each of these chapters is segmented into six sections:

- First, an *overview* of the personality is shared.
- Second, a *short story* will reveal specific characteristics of and scenarios about both the personality type and their co-workers. You will witness the personality type interacting with their co-workers. Those influenced will attempt resolution. From positive outcomes to the less fortuitous results, there is always a lesson to be learned.
- Section Three, *identifying*, will help uncover how to work successfully with this personality. You will find it easy to identify key characteristics of the personality types you work with.
- In Section Four, you'll learn how to *interact* with them. We showcase both positive and negative experiences to help you find common ground and

assist you in applying what you have learned in your current working situation. Interaction in the workplace will be revealed in several ways. You may work for or with the discussed corporate personality. Your interaction with them may be continuous or on a short-term project. The personality that challenges you can be internal or external to the company. Avoiding confrontations and challenging issues with each personality is an area many people struggle with, yet it's one of the most critical elements to maintaining sanity in the workplace.

- In Section Five you'll learn the details of *potential partners* and key *political alliances* of the corporate personality. Knowing *who* to align yourself with and when to make that alignment are important ingredients to career success.

- We focus on how to help you gain a better understanding of the *long-term effects* each personality has on themselves, co-workers, and the company in Section Six.

One important thing to keep in mind: even though the chapters share some minor similarities and thoughts, each personality should be viewed as separate from one another. Their chapters can be read independently and in any order.

We know it's difficult to understand how the game is played, but it's possible. Our work will help you in dealing with, and laughing about, the personality types existing in your work environment. Ultimately this book has been designed to assist you in developing more productive work relationships. You don't have to be a victim of your circumstances.

You may be asking yourself about the book's subtitle, *"Don't Get Caught in the Rally!"* The term rally is defined in tennis as an ongoing return of shots between opponents. In the corporate world, this designates the bandying of a pour soul—the ball—back and forth between corporate personalities. The important thing to remember is,

"Don't get caught in the rally!"

The Players

The Corporate Mutt
(before reading)

The
Workaholic

The
Napoleon

Retired
on the Job

The
Information Hog

Hidden
Agendas

The
Backstabber

The
Spin-Doctor

Acsendo
Inabilitus

The
Corporate Player

The
Gluteus Maximizer

F.A.D.

Exploiting
Talents

The
Cover Up

The
Sour Puss

High Promise,
No Delivery

The
Best of Breed

The
Corporate Ladder

The
Untouchables

The
Know-it-all

The
Micro Manager

The
Court Adviser

The
Gossiper

The
Armchair Manager

The
Ostrich

The
CYA

The Corporate Mutt
(after reading)

The Workaholic
(Too Much Work, Not Enough Time)

The Personality

Corporations today try to be more productive with fewer resources. Many *Workaholics* are created from this environment, as stress becomes the normal state of affairs. The *Workaholic's* effects on the company's bottom line range from the ineffective to the highly productive.

Likewise, there are a few who are driven to work all day and minimize their play. While others create a happy balance of work, social interaction and sustenance, the *Workaholic* is intoxicated with their work and can't kick the habit. Being obsessed with overdoing everything is the passion of some and the slave to others, as this hard working, "get it done" personality doesn't know when to quit.

Some do this out of the desire and will to get ahead. Others are compulsive perfectionists who must see that every detail is completed properly. Those working with and for the *Workaholic* suffer the most, as their lives are filleted at the hand of a professional. Any balance is diminished from their lives as the passionate addict demands total commitment.

The Story

Betty has been working in accounting with Digitron for eight years. She loves her job, but there are just so many beans you can count each day before you go blind. It's five o'clock; enough is enough so she calls it quits for the day. She packs up her belongings and heads for the parking lot. As her aching fifty-year-old body treks its way to the car, she realizes it doesn't make the journey as fast as it used to.

On the way home, she thinks of the many questions people ask about her job. Betty's family and friends, and the general public still ask, "What is a digit?" The question goes unanswered. Just like with other monopolies, the Justice Department investigated Digitron. Still, digit details are vague.

The Company, with many plants throughout the world, is constantly expanding facilities to accommodate the demand for their commercial, industrial, and military digit products. The detailed and armored-finished "Digit Sprocket"—unveiled last week—is the flagship of the Company's new product line.

Her mind then wanders to her boss, Wilfred, who is retiring at the end of the week. There are a lot of people who are sorry to see him go—not because he is such a nice guy and boss, but because he is truly their friend.

The end of the week comes quickly and with a farewell party, Wilfred moves onto greener pastures. He has purchased some land in Montana and is anxious to get his alpaca ranch started. No more early morning meetings! Just throw out some hay, shave those animals twice a year, and let the cash roll in from selling the offspring. What a life!

The following Monday morning, Cletus, the new boss, is introduced. Cletus is a scrappy middle-aged fellow with high ambitions for advancement. He is married with a working wife and no kids. That makes Cletus a D.I.N.K. (Dual Income No Kids).

Cletus loves his job and wants to make a difference. He relishes the thought of reshaping this department into something it has never been: a refined, well-oiled machine. He is determined to make it happen, and to be successful at any cost.

On Wednesday morning, Cletus holds a staff meeting to disclose his new standards of performance. His new policy states that everyone reports to work on time—no matter what—while breaks and lunches are kept to their exact time allowances.

"I will keep my eye on anyone willing to put in any extra time," he thinks.

Since Cletus is a *Workaholic*, he views overtime—without extra pay—as fuel for him to thrive while providing a benefit to the Company.

The next order of business is to increase the quota of financial reports reviewed and the number of audits performed each week. If he can turn out fifteen audits each week, so can everyone else.

"You should feel lucky to be able to work as much as I do," one employee overhears Cletus mumbling to himself.

Cletus believes in running a tight ship with stringent reporting standards and high quotas. These, he believes, comprise the key ingredients to a disciplined group of employees.

"I am sure to get management's attention with this increase of work performance," he thinks.

Everyone, including Betty, is taken aback. Prior to Cletus' arrival, there were zero complaints about this department. In fact, everyone works overtime when necessary without requesting any overtime pay. It's a family type atmosphere where everyone pulls together to get the job done. When time off is needed, it's granted. If extra time at lunch or before work is required, it's accepted. There's a high level of respect and trust in this office. That's what made the old policy work. Department performance used to be measured over a period of a month, but with the new policy a stopwatch will be used to measure all operations.

Betty recalls a scene from the movie *Doc Hollywood* where the nurse clocks the doctor in and out when he reports to and leaves work. The department resembles this mode of operation. In the movie, there was a pig that followed the doctor around. If Cletus' department had a pig, it would feel just like the movie. It's a good thing they don't because the exterminator would have to spray extra around the office with all the food scraps.

Cletus is rigid on his standards and he gives first time offenders a stern talk. It takes only a few falling into this bear trap to signal the others to walk wide of this den of problems. The old heartbeat of the department grows fainter by the day.

Morale has dropped to an all time low. Employees can't remember when things were this bad. Cletus is forcing his passion for work on everyone, and they are beginning to feel like they are working on a chain gang. Manual labor never sounded so good after spending a week under Cletus' regime. Several of the staff are talking of circulating their resume with some of Digitron's competitors. Work has become unbearable and they can't stand their new emperor—the *Workaholic*—and his rigorous approach to business.

People outside the department have heard of Cletus and visualize him as someone who doesn't have a life outside of work. When they hear he is married, they can't believe it.

Later, when they hear the husband and wife are living communally for convenience, they believe this is more realistic and fitting to the person they have heard so much about.

Other departments within Digitron picture Cletus standing on a pedestal with a long whip in hand, driving the serfs—his staff—to work harder and produce more. Some imagine receiving a lump of coal for the holidays instead of a yearly bonus in return for a hard year's work. Bah humbug!

Cletus loves to compare his results and work output to others by showing off how much he can do in relation to them.

"Betty, how many audits have you completed this week?" Cletus demands.

"Three so far," she says.

"Well, I have five completed," he snidely replies.

He always produces two or three more audits than Betty. Through his snide remarks and the tone of his voice he ensures she feels like she has been crapped on by a flock of wild turkeys.

"Hey, wait a minute," she thinks. "Turkeys can't fly." She learned that by watching an old episode of *WKRP*. "Change that to uh um... I am going to have to go study my birds."

Cletus is driving the department into the dust with his slave-driving standards and snide remarks. People are leaving and morale is falling right off the cliff. Things have never looked worse.

Betty tries to boost morale by having group discussions with several of the staff in the lunchroom during breaks. She wants everyone to work this out so that Cletus doesn't totally destroy the life they had prior to his dictatorship. Talking about a problem objectively always helps. It's better to fully understand it rather than bottling it up and having sideline chit chat discussions that seem to only fuel the issue. It will help the group to get together, discuss their problems, and share what they don't like about these changes. Betty suggests they write down this information to have a clear understanding of the issues. This will help them learn to cope with these changes.

They document what has changed both positively and negatively in their department. They also note their work performance prior to Cletus' arrival and compare it to current production. In addition, they detail employee turnover and the intense learning curve the "new bodies," filling the vacant slots, must master. Since Cletus expects consistent output, the old timers will have to make up the slack for the newbies that are just learning.

"Why not put electronic collars on everyone?" Betty thinks.

After they work on their report for several weeks, Betty decides to share it with Claude, the director of finance. She knows him well and respects his judgment, so she telephones him to make an appointment.

"Hello Claude, this is Betty. Are you available for a few minutes? I have something I would like to discuss with you."

"This is a good time to come over if you can," he replies.

"I am flying out the door right now," she says.

Betty hurries to Claude's office to explain the situation to him. She is so happy to have some compassionate discussion on this issue.

"I knew that Cletus made some changes when he took over, but I had no idea they were so severe," he states. "Things seem to be spiraling out of control. I will have a chat with him."

Betty thanks him for his time and returns to her workstation.

Claude has a talk with Cletus to discuss department changes. He realizes that Cletus' motives are all about pleasing upper management. Cletus expects everyone to put in as much time as he does in getting the job done. If he were just an employee, this extreme work ethic would be tolerable. Since he is a manager, he holds the same level of expectations for everyone in his department as he does for himself. That's a good attribute, but he is going overboard with his unrealistic demands.

Just when Claude is planning to consult with other directors in the Company for advice on how to handle the Cletus situation, things work themselves out. The IRS pays a little visit to Cletus' office. It seems that Cletus has been doing overtime auditing on his income taxes and a personal business he ran last year. There's a lot of money missing from the government coffers based on some creative accounting practices Cletus employed. The department's in awe as Cletus is led away in handcuffs.

The department gets together to discuss what has happened. The primary lesson they have learned is that things are not always what they seem to be. Cletus seemed to be a well-organized, driven individual who wanted to impose his ambitions on those in his department. No one would ever guess he was manipulating his contributions to the government.

A few months later, the department learns that Cletus is provided an all-expenses-paid trip to Leavenworth where he can crack his whip all day and others will enjoy it. Now he will have time to reorganize another group and perhaps they will read or hear about him on the news: "Inmate makes new friends during reorganization."

Identifying

The two types of *Workaholics* are "highly productive," and "useless busyness." Both types crave the inebriation of work. To determine if you are working with or for a *Workaholic*, look for these indicators:

- Constantly works long hours
- Exhibits sense of urgency to do work
- Engages in few hobbies or outside interests other than work
- Talks of their love and passion in life—their work
- Measures their work ethic and results against others

This personality may contain some or all of the above specific traits. However, more subtle behaviors and attributes may include high intensity levels, exceedingly high stress, anger, or apparent frustration with less-than-desirable work performance (or time commitment) from employees.

Interaction

If you happen to have a *Workaholic* as your direct boss or as another manager you interact with, you may have a challenging time enjoying your job. Shouting and stress flow freely under the regime of this personality. Caution is advised for these conditions as the *Workaholic* will enforce their authority and invoke discipline for questioning it. Seek group opinion, after you have properly documented the details of the issue—just as Betty did—and consult with a trusted manager who isn't involved in the situation. You will obtain honest feedback and support to remedy the circumstances.

If the personality is a co-worker and interaction is necessary, then document behaviors and approach your manager with the situation. Confrontation isn't advised as these hard workers are viewed as workhorses in the organization. Therefore, threats to their production could jeopardize more than your interaction with them. Their contribution could be supporting many managers within the organization. Remember, these individuals are passionate about their work and any threatened changes will have them fighting for their enjoyed environment.

Partners/Political Alliances

Workaholics can choose to partner with each other as they find solace in those they respect. They respect high output, attention to details, and an extraordinary level of work quality. From their perspective, others who choose to have a life outside of work are missing out on getting things done—there's too much work to get done and not enough time to do it.

They will sometimes partner with an authority figure if their goals are to move up in an organization. *Napoleons* love them—*Workaholics* are a twenty-four hour by seven-day army plowing through the empire hurdles.

Long-term Effects

Workaholics careers can have a varied outcome. If they are reserved and push only themselves to a high work ethic, then little conflict arises and they are looked upon as committed, valuable employees. *Workaholics* will be promoted and may make good managers if they don't impose unrealistic expectations on staff.

Problems are encountered when *Workaholics* force their unrelenting drive on others. They may burn bridges as well as challenge co-workers and their staff to the point of becoming an isolated island. Should this personality continue down this path, they could encounter team mutiny. Ethical management who looks upon unnecessary games and competitions as morale killers can become involved to restrain this personality.

Although this personality can have significant contributions to a corporation's bottom line, over time the *Workaholic* faces burnout. How long can they keep going at this pace without becoming exhausted from overwork?

Workaholics have many motives for their behavior that include personal success, power, money and recognition. If a *Workaholic* is sponsored by a deposed *Napoleon* or other corporate personality, then their future may be bleak and they will have to jockey for a new sponsor quickly.

8:35 on a Christmas Eve.

Jack Campbell still at his desk.

Now there's a hallmark moment for you.

The Family Man

First prize is a new car.

Second prize is a set of steak knives.

Third prize is you're fired!

Glengarry Glen Ross

The Napoleon
(The Empire Builder)

The Personality

Some workers have a relentless thirst to rule an empire. They are driven to create, appoint administrators, govern, and reshape—as needed—this kingdom of theirs. Kingdoms come in many flavors. A fiefdom to one is an empire to another. A new project can bring out the ruler in some, where having control of a staff of many is the necessity of others. In dealing with these people, it's good to remember their underlying belief: it's their kingdom so don't get in their way.

Many times this road to glory is paved with good intentions, but their ideals stray from the corporation's goals. This can wreak havoc for employees and the company. Because they hide in the performance of the past and statements of the present and future, many don't see the *Napoleons* for who they are. Only through close examination does this corporate personality reveal itself. This leads some to say from far away it looks like a Monet, but up close it's a big old mess.

The Story

Susan, a new project manager assigned to the West Coast office of Digitron, is ready to get her feet wet and meet her co-workers. She is a tall, slender woman in her mid-thirties, with long brown hair and a pleasant smile. With a sensible head for business, she always observes situations first before making conclusions, and most importantly, taking action.

Out on a walk to meet her new co-workers, she looks up to see Mike, the area vice president, heading her way. Mike's reputation precedes him. She has heard he rules with an iron fist and only tolerates success. It's his way or the highway. There's no room for discussion, as others have learned the hard way and are added to the list of corporate world casualties.

Susan has seen a lot of casualties—sometimes referred to as victims—in her years of service both at Digitron and previous companies. One victim she remembers is Plinka from East Germany. This rather stout woman believed in hard work and no play. She was caught in a large game rally—a corporate game—in Digitron's Eastern European plant.

It seems Plinka was convinced goo preservation—part of the digit making process—was a high priority and made sure only adequate amounts were used in production. Her boss, Rusticoff, had a goo business on the side and large amounts of the ingredient were missing each month. When Plinka started to investigate, she was met head on by a *Gluteus Maximizer* who positioned strategic smooches in the division. She never expected support for the *Napoleon* (Rusticoff) and was blindsided. It seemed Rusticoff used this support personality to obtain additional power and authority in exchange for his other deeds. Plinka found herself heading home rather quickly after challenging such a masked regime. Susan reminds herself to tread lightly until she can determine who the players are in this new office.

Mike, a short, well-rounded individual with thick, wavy hair and an arrogant air, walks up and greets her. He is polite while introducing himself and starts explaining how he likes things run.

"I like my people to focus on success and to have their respective departments exceed the goals of all other counterparts in the Company," he proudly states.

Susan looks him in the eye. "I am an overachiever myself," she replies. Without saying a word, he gives her a look of agreement and is off to another meeting.

She has talked with several people in her new office and understands the Corporate objectives for this area. Mike is nice and polite, but maintains himself as a figurehead of authority. She notices this when another employee interrupts their conversation and Mike immediately takes control. He seems to want every employee to take note of him. Based on his arrogance, she almost expects some to bow as he enters a room.

She has heard of people like this, called *Napoleons*. They want control over everything in their kingdom. Since they are empire builders, they can be anyone from the head of a corporation all the way down to someone just managing a process. Their kingdom is as they see and create it.

The next day, Susan receives an email to come to Mike's office at 3:00 p.m. When she arrives, she has to wait outside for thirty minutes as a bustle of activity is taking place before her. Several people are bringing in papers as others hurriedly exit his office with laptops, organizers, and papers in tow. This reminds her of the activity surrounding a politician in the midst of a culminating campaign. Finally it's her turn to see Mike. He greets her with excitement and asks what she has been spending her time on.

"What has been your focus these last few days, Susan?" Mike inquires.

"I've been organizing the rollout of the Deep Space Digit," Susan replies. It's a waste of time answering this question, because Mike glosses over the reply and states what's on his mind.

"I want you to start organizing the projects in this office and ensure they exceed any other region's performance," he firmly states.

He thanks her and is again surrounded by a herd of people fighting for his time. She sees herself to the door and ponders what she has just witnessed.

"Mike's comments are very different than how I see my job," she wonders. "In fact, they are very different than any of my peers in the Company. It seems he has other plans for me since I am in his kingdom. It appears he has transformed the Corporate goals into his own, and has mutated them to become his objective."

She observes the staff working for Mike as just bodies. A quote from the movie *Superman II* comes to mind. " I can't have you with me if you are not with me." If all of the staff are not on board with all of the objectives of the *Napoleon*, then they are perceived as not being full team players in his eyes. "Expendable" is a common word attached to their staff (or should we say subjects?). For non-team players the punishment is banishment, a lesson administered often by the *Napoleon*. Even though customers, both internal and external, may not be serviced in the best manner due to the *Napoleon's* empire building, this ruler overlooks customers to achieve their own objective. In fact, the staff that modifies their behavior to accommodate their customer's needs and creates any violation of the *Napoleon's* objective are subject to strict criticism.

Susan also notices Mike isn't as tall as the others on his staff. Standing five foot eight inches, she's in fact taller than Mike. "Give this guy the right clothes and a box to stand on and he could rule," she thinks.

She has witnessed Mike wants to be involved in most decisions. While she was in his office, his phone rang no less than five times and three people were knocking at his door to obtain his stamp of approval on various projects. "It's the control factor *Napoleons* love," she thinks. This approach gives those working for the *Napoleon* all the responsibility with minimal authority. Any authority has to be earned, and it's only delegated to those who uphold the *Napoleon's* objectives. "Get me someone on the phone, and get me someone while I am waiting," Susan recalls from *National Lampoon's Christmas Vacation*. It's a feeling of importance they strive to create around them.

She knows it's imperative to perform her job according to Corporate's expectations, but she must also work within the *Napoleon's* guidelines. Rocking the boat could be a career disaster on her part. Mike has a lot of power, and she has to respect it.

Susan decides to sit down and write two lists: her Corporate goals, and Mike's empire goals he shared with her. She compares the two lists and records the differences. She imagines the office is full of serfs carrying sticks and dressed in rags all to serve the king. She will focus on adapting herself to work on these differences between the Corporate and the empire builder's missions. The one thing she won't tolerate is having customers suffer, so she outlines a plan that complements the *Napoleon's* mission, provides a high level of service to customers, and provides the necessary support she needs out of the staff.

She takes this plan to Mike and asks for his signoff. This will ensure her mission is endorsed by the reigning monarchy and her job is fairly safe. She wants to minimize any surprises.

Upon arriving at Mike's office, her first thought is to ask him to stand to greet her, but she realizes he is standing. She has to get over this "little man's syndrome" issue with such a powerful ruler. Susan presents her plan to Mike, and after making some adjustments, he signs off on it. "Now is the time to implement and conquer—proceed," she thinks.

She works diligently with all parameters in mind. She finds both respect and praise from the staff and Mike. Susan is contributing heavily to the office, and even Corporate feels she is making a real difference. It's the *balance* her plan contains that is helping her through this. Mike feels Susan is serving his kingdom, and she is maintaining good rapport with Corporate at the same time. It's a tightrope, and she is walking it well.

Tolerance also helps Susan though this. She has to muster great restraint so she doesn't scream at meetings with the *Napoleon* where *Gluteus Maximizers*, *Ascendo Inabilituses*, and others play their games with him. It's like being in a den of psychotic thieves. Don't turn your back; sit facing out from a corner like Wild Bill Hickcock.

Susan works in the office for another two years, but only six months of that time is spent with Mike around. He is asked to relocate his office to Nome, Alaska. It seems that one of the *Gluteus Maximizers* let out too much information, and Corporate caught wind of how Mike is running his kingdom. His dictatorship violates many Corporate policies, so he is banished to a more remote digit-producing facility.

Perhaps he can set up a kingdom with the grizzly bears?

Identifying

The *Napoleon* is the empire builder. This powerful ruler creates his or her own kingdom and demands total allegiance from the subjects they control. To identify this leader, look for these ruling characteristics:

- Creates own kingdom
- Establishes monarchy rules that stray from the corporate directive
- Rules with an iron fist
- Is extremely driven
- Demands strict punishment for those who don't follow the empire rules
- Has own objective in mind and all subjects serve to achieve it
- Is results-minded
- Exhibits little regard for employees
- Appears to be in a constant flurry of activity
- Attracts other personalities trading their supreme allegiance for favors
- Uses power to influence others in personal kingdom

Interaction

You will realize after identifying the *Napoleon* that resistance is futile. It's important to maintain a good working relationship and work within the parameters set forth by this personality. To accomplish this, you must have a clear understanding of the *Napoleon's* expectations and execute them as accurately as possible.

Also keep in mind *Napoleons* tend to be trendsetters and pioneers while welcoming new ideas and suggestions. If you contribute an idea to their empire and it's not used, move on and don't dwell on the possible disappointment.

Napoleons' strengths are the passion for success and the motivation to pioneer new ideas. They are drivers for getting things done. In some instances, projects and assignments will be completed in a timely fashion only with them at the helm.

Partners/Political Alliances

Napoleons will partner with their kind. The sharing of authority and power draws these personalities to one another. Additionally, they need overachievers to carry out their missions, so they solicit alliances with all who can help their cause.

Napoleons won't like *Retired on the Job*, the *Corporate Player*, the *Best of Breed*, *F.A.D.*, the *Sour Puss*, and the *Gossiper*. These personalities don't possess the drive and support this empire builder needs in their kingdom. Likewise, the *Napoleon* won't associate with other authority figures that run their kingdoms strictly by the corporate directive. Operations of these kinds could threaten the very foundation of this ruler's monarchy.

Personalities who gravitate towards the *Napoleon* include the *Spin-Doctor*, *Ascendo Inabilitus*, the *Gluteus Maximizer*, the *Corporate Ladder*, the *Workaholic*, and the *Micro Manager*. Each of these personalities wants to attract the attention of this ruler to provide a service to their kingdom in return for a future favor.

Long-term Effects

Napoleons live on the edge. If they can create a successful empire and work within the guidelines of the corporate politics, they may carve out a long-term niche. This leads to significant corporate contributions and the pioneering of new ideas within an organization.

However, if *Napoleons* aren't able to balance their own ideas with their corporate directive and blend them into the corporation's main objectives, they may find themselves being offered a lower position—or a severance package—during company reorganizations. Many can't handle this balance and find their way to the royal graveyards as another casualty in the corporate world.

One thing that *Napoleons* don't consider are the potential lawsuits, PR issues and public opinion of companies that allow rogue managers to rule their own kingdoms. Too many times they aren't aware of anyone but themselves. The company has to mop up the financial mess that may place serious burdens on them for quite some time.

I am big, you're little,
and there's nothing you can do about it.

Matilda

Retired on the Job
(Doing as Little as Possible)

The Personality

To trade a service for compensation—a definition of work for most of us—many people are compelled to do their best. Their drive isn't just to satisfy their employer, but to know personally they performed a job well done, with fair compensation for services rendered.

Still, there are those who just want to get by, doing as little as possible. This can be for a variety of reasons—complacency, insecurity, even anger. These deterrents to productivity originate from this personality's bad experience in the corporate world.

Many corporations have these personalities working in their tranquil, secluded, niche serving their time quietly before they move on to another company or, if possible, retire. Meet *Retired on the Job*.

The Story

Phil reports to his cube for another long, monotonous day of staring wide-eyed at his computer parked just twelve inches from his nose. He isn't known for his ambition, excitement or emotion—just the lack of. Phil is thirty pounds overweight and appears to have slept in his clothes. His tousled hair and two-day growth of beard has this unhealthy looking fifty-something- man appearing to be in sad shape. He spends day after day in the office fixated on his PC. Employees walk by his cube and believe they see sunlight glistening off the drool coming from the corner of his mouth.

Every day is like Friday to Phil. When 5:00 p.m. arrives, the rubber meets the road as he makes a beeline for the parking lot. Because Phil is without passion (except at 5:00 p.m.), many wonder if he's lazy, shy, carefree, or retired. He's a recluse, seen only during his numerous trips to the snack machine. "How can anyone live on Twinkies?" many think as he is seen bringing his catch back to his cube.

Karen is a new employee in sales support. Petite and small-framed with short dark hair, she's been assigned to work with Phil on a special project. Management believes her pleasant demeanor and vivid enthusiasm will wake Phil from his stupor and get some work out of him. It's time Phil pulled his load, so co-workers aren't motivated to place a mirror under his nose to see if he's still alive. The project involves examining sales-prospecting success and determining how to improve it. This, in return, will generate more business for the Company.

Karen is an astute woman and does her homework on Phil before she meets him and starts the project. Co-workers wonder just what Phil's problem is. His lack of association has some placing bets on how long he will last in the company. Others play practical jokes on him. Just the other day, another co-worker loaded a program on Phil's computer—when he was out on a Twinkie run—that made typed characters fall off the screen and pile up at the bottom. From their observations, Phil didn't even notice the joke. Karen knows there's more to Phil's situation than has been witnessed. She observes Phil for a few days and takes note of his actions—or lack thereof.

Phil wanders into the office late and heads for his cube. The computer is turned on, his feet go up, and he just stares into space. The in-box is overloaded; while his out-box has cobwebs on it. This reminds Karen of the movie *Office Space:*

"I come in around 9:15 and sneak in the back way so Lumbergh doesn't see me. Then I just space out...You know just stare at my computer or wall for an hour or so ... I would say I only do maybe fifteen minutes of real work each week... It's not that I'm lazy, I'm just not motivated."

That's exactly how Karen sees Phil: not motivated. She wouldn't be surprised if Phil came in one day with a Hawaiian shirt on, erected a hammock in his cube, and then climbed into it and napped all day.

Karen cares about the Company and the money it wastes on needless items. It could mean a bigger raise or better benefits for her if she does her part to ensure anything she can influence is accomplished wisely and efficiently. She is determined to "flush out the demons" in Phil and see what happens. (Of course this isn't going to be an exorcism, just a challenge on Phil's part to stay awake and take an active part in an assignment.)

It's Wednesday morning. Phil has just settled into a nice snooze parked in his caster-laden reclining hammock. Susan walks into his cube and before she can say anything, hears the gentle "zzzzz" as he snores his way through the day. She walks around to face him, and realizes he's sleeping with his eyes open. While others spend time learning about a new product or writing a report, Phil has spent his time mastering the art of the corporate siesta. Fuel for the practical joker would be to tug on the fire alarm—whose siren is just above Phil's cube—or create some other loud noise to wake him abruptly from his slumber.

Karen loudly clears her throat, and Phil revives back to a conscious state to rejoin the Digitron workforce. As he starts to destroy "The Sandman's" work, Susan delivers the details of their new assignment. Phil gives her a glance that says, "You've got to be kidding," but she continues. His face reads, "Go away and leave me alone," so a determined Karen presses on.

She coaxes him out of his cube to a conference room with a Twinkie. Karen starts reviewing her perspective of the project with him.

"Now, we are a team and it's going to take participation from both of us to make this project successful," she states. "You have a background in prospecting, and I have sales closing skills. Together we can complete this project correctly and make a difference."

She notices Phil is slumped in his chair with a sour look on his face.

"This is just like waking a child up early to go to school," she thinks. She searches through her mind for ways to motivate Phil. "I had a former boss who motivated his people with a cattle prod," she chuckles to herself. "A little too harsh and non-motivating in any situation."

After a few bites of the Twinkie, Phil comes back to life.

"I am really having a hard time seeing the benefit of this project for me," he says.

"Digitron offers a paycheck in return for your time and effort; correct?" she says to Phil.

"Yes, I guess so," he replies.

"With a new round of corporate layoffs projected, I would like to be able to share your value on this project with management. I wouldn't wish for anyone to be laid off, but I have to be honest with management when they inquire about participation on this project," she states.

That gets Phil's attention. He straightens himself in his chair.

"Phil, knowing we have to prospect to be successful, tell me more about your approach," she says.

"I hope and pray the next call I make is a 'yes' or someone is even remotely nice to me on the phone. I really struggle with rejection," he replies.

It appears to Karen that Phil needs encouragement and support. This is needed not only on this project, but also regarding his work in general. Karen surmises his lack of ambition results from insecurity and complacency out of a lack of caring. Phil did comment he hates rejection. She has witnessed his complacent attitude. She has to get him motivated.

Karen encourages Phil to share his thoughts and ideas for this project. She has heard the one who is most flexible in a situation is the one in control. Karen notices Phil is starting to open up more and contribute to their project.

After a busy week of working with Phil, she even convinces him to stay a few extra hours after work. The two complete the prospecting project in the allotted timeframe. Phil is starting to see how focusing on performance can be very satisfying, and this gives him more confidence.

Identifying

The real key to recognizing *Retired on the Job* is to take the needed time to assess the situation and behavior displayed. Unique attributes are:

- Catnaps in cube
- Allows in-box to become stacked high with overdue materials

- May mount hammock in corner of office
- Lacks excitement or motivation about new job assignment
- Tends to produce late or incomplete work

If you can spend the extra time to recognize and identify the above characteristics, you will have more success in working with *Retired on the Job*. Relating and understanding this personality type will assist you in motivating them.

The positives to this personality are few and far between. Still, what may lie before you is a slumbering capable contributor. If you are able to motivate them, *Retired on the Job* may be able to exert their unique perspective on a company project and could contribute in a positive manner.

Interaction

Interacting with *Retired on the Job* requires flexibility and a delicate approach. Many people may make a show of excitement or energy in hopes of leading this personality by example, but this overcompensation tends to overwhelm *Retired on the Job*. This will only lead to frustration and a lack of productivity from both parties. Effort is best spent encouraging *Retired on the Job* to do most of the talking. From this you will find some common interests. Then you can use the connection to work towards a successful relationship.

Retired on the Job will rarely cause conflict. If confronted, they resemble a turtle and pull back into their own world. Virtually zero work can be accomplished if they are pushed out of their comfort zone.

Partners/Political Alliances

Retired on the Job will have very few, if any, political alliances. As you are now aware, this personality won't participate in team projects unless a common goal is set. If you are a manager, encountering this personality will help you in developing your career by bringing the best out of this unmotivated worker. If you motivate them, you will have formed a strong working partnership, and the lessons you've both learned can be used for future situations.

Long-term Effects

If you form a common bond with *Retired on the Job,* this will lead to a positive outcome. This will also encourage them to share many of their ideas, resulting in beneficial contribution to the company.

However, if this personality remains in their shell, they will be hiding their underachievement. This may result in disciplinary action or unemployment. Take time to assess the situation and personality involved. They are even-tempered with low excitement levels, so being overzealous will push *Retired on the Job* away.

I dunno man.
That sounds like a lot of work.

American Pie

The Information Hog
(Hoarding Information for Job Security)

The Personality

From when we were very little, our parents, teachers, and friends taught us to share. In the corporate world, some people feel sharing creates vulnerability and hoarding is beneficial. This personality clutches to their precious information as if it were gold, and they let others take a peek only when necessary. *Information Hogs* hoard in proportion to their information resource competition. That way, they can create a high value for themselves based on the information they possess. In these circumstances, the information they have becomes exclusive and other sources can't obtain it.

Working with this personality can be a challenge, although their participation in group settings and projects may reveal the information they hoard. The *Information Hog* is more amenable to sharing if the requester can offer information in exchange so there is reciprocation of data.

The Story

Ron knows from experience shortcuts rarely work and finding "The Way" is like discovering the Holy Grail. For three years he has worked for Digitron. Now in a new technical support position, he strives to be the best—a perfectionist at heart. Perfection and pride are masters Ron strives to quench the thirst of each day.

He is proud to work with such a prestigious worldwide corporation that produces many digit types. Ron wants to be associated with a leader and his quest has ended at Digitron. This Company was founded on principles of build-it-right-the-first-time, so every digit from the smallest intricate part up to large military versions are stringently inspected for quality. Ron must intelligently support all products. He hears that his peer Jeff, in the Mud Flats plant, is the subject matter expert (SME) on digits.

Jeff, a five-year Digitron veteran, maintains a high level of digit product knowledge. He prides himself on fielding any technical question and is constantly bettering himself on existing and new product details. Jeff also waits anxiously for the parking lot to be paved. With every rain, waders are required to safely negotiate the mud to the front door. After one of Mud Flats' famous downpours, the dry hard dusty surface transforms into a sea of thick brown mud. It clings to shoes and any surface that comes in contact with it. "Bring-your-dog-to-work-day" is impossible with the unpredictable weather. To make matters worse, more severe parking lot problems have been known to occur. Rumor has it James in production lost his Datsun in the parking lot after a thunder-storm overwhelmed the plant. The resulting mud just opened up, swallowed his car, and it was never seen again. Jeff under-stands these are not just local parking lot issues because Digitron focuses on products and not frivolous amenities like fields of asphalt. No wonder the plant was given the name it bears.

Because of his passion to be an expert in product knowl-edge, Ron always seeks the best resource and decides to contact Jeff. After a detailed telephone discussion, the two determine it's best for Ron to make a trip to see Jeff and learn more about products. Because digits are so complex in nature, hands-on experience is the best way for one to learn the de-tails of these products. Ron starts securing the necessary approvals and purchases tickets. Then, out of nowhere, Jeff calls and cancels the trip. He no longer has time to dedicate to Ron's training. Ron probes for answers, but Jeff evades the attempts and doesn't explain further.

"This is weird," Ron thinks. "All this time and effort to plan my trip, and now things are cancelled." He ponders the words Jeff concluded his cancellation notice with. "Perhaps you can get this information from someone at our Corporate office?"

Ron wants to learn more about Jeff in order to uncover what could have caused this reversal in plans. He learns from other employees that Jeff hoards information, doesn't volun-tarily share, discusses what is needed with the requester off-line, and rarely speaks up in group settings. Ron feels strongly about going to the best information source and doesn't give up easily. Little setbacks like these can drive workers mad and send them off in a flurry of anger and frustration. But not Ron: he is determined to learn from the best.

In his last position, Ron recalls a similar occurrence involving Hereford, a fellow worker. Hereford was working with another colleague to obtain information on a product and his situation took a similar track. His change in plans apparently upset Hereford greatly and caused a display of emotion. (He shouldn't have thrown his laptop across the room.) That action put him in a lot of trouble with his manager and the IT department. Ron observed how Hereford reacted to this quandary, so he is taking a different approach to his own situation. Causing controversy or having an emotional fit over a cancelled trip isn't something Ron wants to do. He decides to seek advice from his former boss, Rufus, to understand this personality better before taking any action.

Rufus is a stodgy, experienced fellow, with a scruffy beard and a "tell it like it is" attitude. His oddity is collecting stuffed parakeets, even though others find the shelf based peering birds eerie. He finds fascination with these colorful birds, and with the stuffed version there isn't worry about noise or escape. Most people are distracted by this odd collection on the shelves in Rufus' office, but not Ron. He's on a mission to uncover details on how to work with such a personality. There are no holds barred with Rufus, so Ron prepares to get an earful.

Rufus welcomes the questions and listens intently as Ron explains the situation with Jeff.

"It sounds like Jeff is an *Information Hog,*" the veteran manager states. "*Hogs* feel that some day their job may be in jeopardy or the information they possess has higher importance than that of anyone else. Because of this, they often feel more marketable, which could lead them to a promotion or other Corporate benefit. This makes this personality less willing to part with information they think makes them more valuable."

With this description, Ron imagines a hog faced person off in the corner cuddling lots of information. The *Hogs* hoard this information for their own use and purpose. He chuckles about this visual, even though he knows creating mental images like this may develop into a negative attitude.

Rufus continues with his analysis. "*Hogs* are usually created because someone stole one of their ideas and used it for
personal or corporate gain." Rufus details how this personality behaves and some of the environmental influences. "They
could have been passed over for a promotion, or even been
released from a company, due to someone else's theft or mis-
representation of their idea. The boss may see someone else's
value to be greater than the *Information Hog's*. This leaves
them feeling betrayed and drives them to hoard ideas so they
are the only information resource. They create a self-perceived
value and believe they are irreplaceable."

"*Information Hogs* evaluate how many other information
sources can challenge their knowledge. The hoarding factor is
dependent on two main points:

- First is the **type of company** for which they work. A
  small company with limited resources creates a valuable *Hog* where many seek answers to their questions.
  They become the sole source for information. Larger
  companies drive the *Hog* to increase their hoarding
  factor in proportion to the information resource competition. They withhold information by reducing access to
  knowledge their resource competition could access to
  become more knowledgeable. Thus, they increase their
  own value.
- Second is the **industry type**. High tech industries
  often have specialized people to support products and
  services. In other industries, limited resource competition minimizes hoarding while any potential or realized
  changes in company structure can increase it."

"This is very interesting and helpful," Ron thinks. He
thanks Rufus for this wisdom and retires to a quiet place to
think more about this corporate personality and what his next
steps should be.

"It may be best to get to know Jeff," Ron considers. Experience has taught him that breaking down barriers and earning
trust with a co-worker is much better than taking the brute
force method of trying to wring the information out of them. If
they share willingly, the information is considered genuine.

Ron remembers there is going to be a group meeting in two weeks at Corporate headquarters. Jeff and Ron are both scheduled to attend and this will be a perfect time to start building trust. Ron may discover what makes Jeff tick, his past, and some information on how to work with him better in the future.

"Some people may seek revenge for a situation like this," Ron ponders. "After all, I had to scramble to work around this informational set back. No one likes to change directions completely without reason when all parties agreed to set the wheels in motion to achieve the defined goal. " Ron realizes a different approach is called for, not just because it's the right thing to do, but also because he will make a new friend and have a valuable resource he can count on.

The meeting day arrives and he asks if Jeff wants to get together for a beer after the group dinner that evening. Jeff welcomes the invitation with a slight smile, so they set a time and place to meet.

Over an ice cold, frosty beer in a smoke-filled bar, the two share small talk before Ron inquires about Jeff's past positions. He wants to learn about his career and confirm Jeff's depth of product knowledge. Ron ignores the need for more oxygen as two well-fed gentlemen settle nearby and fire up their Cubans.

Jeff starts to open up and share some of his past. "In my last company, someone stole one of my ideas and received a promotion over me because of it" Jeff comments. "Since then, I am reluctant to get involved in what others are doing."

With Jeff's enthusiastic tone and the excitement in his hand motions— or was he just waving smoke out of the area— Ron senses Jeff wants to help, but past experience really haunts him and puts the governors on the amount of information he shares.

Ron shows empathy for Jeff's experiences by listening, acknowledging, and relating a similar series of events from his previous job.

"When a woman in the design department took credit for inventing the Brain Buster—a toy that was eventually banned by the government due to over-tweaking people's melons—the actual idea and development person nearly lost it," Ron replies. "He withdrew and worked quietly in a back office for several months until he took another, less meaningful job. I'm glad you didn't go that direction. You seem to be a team player as long as you feel part of the team. Am I right?"

Jeff concurs with Ron's statement.

As the two continue to chat about their careers at Digitron, Jeff seems more open to work with Ron. A bond of trust begins to form, as it does with any budding acquaintance or friendship. From Jeff's observations, Ron appears to be genuine and not some hack on his way through the system.

Jeff explains he wants information sharing to be a two-way street. Otherwise, he is supporting other's jobs. It makes him feel like Rodney Dangerfield: "I get no respect." That's an important point, and Ron picks up on it.

Ron glances at his gold-plated Timex watch and realizes it's getting late. "The meetings start early tomorrow and I need my beauty rest," Ron comments. Jeff agrees and the two leave the bar smelling like they have been rolling around in an ashtray.

Mid-afternoon the next day, the meeting ends and everyone heads home. Ron remembers to make information sharing a two-way street, so he spends the time to find out some of the areas that Jeff is lacking in knowledge.

Ron can't just casually look up some information and share it with Jeff. He has to spend time learning the information so he knows it well and can teach Jeff. This review brings back some memories from college. "You have to know information to properly teach it," is what Ron most remembers about Professor Olsen from those years in college. A tag-team approach to information sharing will have both of them up to speed on all technical information relating to Digitron products.

Ron starts taking the initiative. He becomes a resident expert on several new areas of information, documenting and preparing to share with Jeff. On top of the cultivation of the relationship with Jeff as a resource, Ron is increasing his value through product information, as well as learning where the knowledge bases are throughout the Company.

After a few weeks, Ron phones Jeff to share with him some of the products and their respective details he has recently learned. Jeff realizes the benefits from a two-way informational sharing session with Ron, unlike the relationships others have pursued. They reschedule their meeting and Jeff comments to Ron, "pray it doesn't rain when you visit." Ron looks puzzled, but brushes it off to an inside joke he will learn more about later.

Ron flies out to see Jeff, spends a day and a half exchanging information with him, and in the end both agree it has been a productive session. Both are more knowledgeable and know in the future they can call upon each other for information without reserve. In the long run, Digitron benefits from this knowledge sharing so that islands of information are minimized, cross training is achieved, and there are multiple sources for valuable information.

Identifying

For you to have success identifying the *Information Hog* personality, it's best to gain a better understanding of the key attributes of this corporate personality type. Although some characteristics are generalities, there are some distinct qualities you will notice when interacting with this personality.

A winning approach is to identify with and recognize these key identifiers. For the *Information Hog*, these include:

- Keeps to self—unwilling to share with others
- Is usually an expert in a specific technical area
- Shares only when forced or a self-benefit is at stake
- Is reluctant to open up during company meetings
- May carry an attitude of "company can't exist without me and the knowledge I possess"

As you may have noticed in the story, Jeff initially was willing to share information, but then became very reluctant to part with any of his time or knowledge.

Interaction

You can have successful interaction with the *Information Hog*. The first step to this success is proper identification by looking for the key characteristics as outlined earlier. Just as a tracker learns to identify an animal by its trails, you will learn to identify corporate personalities by the tracks they leave. Once you know with whom you are working, you can better adjust your approach to work with this corporate personality.

The next step to a successful work relationship with this personality is to lead by example. If you can share both personal and professional information about yourself, the *Hog* will begin to trust you and open up. An important point to remember is the information must be genuine and sincere. If the *Hog* senses you are trying to be manipulative to pry information, shut down will occur. Challenging and forcing this personality to divulge information is futile. Although they rarely get hostile, you will experience conflict if your tack is manipulative or forceful. In these cases *Hogs* develop a case of lockjaw and, because of their backgrounds, you rarely get a second chance to earn trust. Remember, the *Information Hog* shares information based on comfort level and perception of personal gain. If you can initiate a level of confidence that the relationship will be a two-way learning experience, this personality will be prone to sharing.

Partners/Political Alliances

Information Hogs normally align themselves with non-threatening alliances in addition to authority figures who can further their career. This personality doesn't want to be an isolationist, but they feel forced to hoard information based on their past experiences.

In many organizations, the *Hog* runs rampant. They stash information to be used another day. In some cases they have been known to use this power to work with many of the other players defined in this work.

Long-term Effects

Just how open *Information Hogs* are to sharing and easing their hoarding with you, will determine their overall career success. When you are able to create a successful working relationship, there is valuable knowledge exchange. In the long run everyone wins—including you, the *Hog*, and the company.

If *Hogs* choose to continuously isolate themselves and appear as total hoarders of information, they are viewed as a limited resource. Their value to the company is diminished, as they have become restrictive *Hogs* that absorb and hoard information. When *Hogs* reach this state they are referred to as the *"Diode Information Hog,"* as information flows only one way with this unique member of the swine family.

Hidden Agendas
(Do as I Want, Not as I Say)

The Personality

Agendas are like opinions; everyone has one. Some agendas are clear and well defined, while others are kept concealed. Agendas that are kept secret most likely violate the corporate directive and strictly benefit the owner.

Working with a new boss or co-worker brings opportunity as well as challenges to the working environment. Observation of the workplace, careful reaction to situations, and well thought-out strategies for a win-win outcome are necessary for an employee to thrive.

Those that mask their agendas resemble a thief hiding their intent. We call these personalities *Hidden Agendas*.

The Story

Ken reports to his new position as technology consultant at the Nome, Alaska branch of Digitron. This is a big change for this southerner, but Ken is now literally at the top of the world. He is used to a more temperate latitude, humidity so thick you can cut it, and fried pickles.

The harsh winter languishes as spring nips at the snow and ice, taking little bites every day. Each day lingers briefly from the previous as Ken spends time getting acclimated with the plant and employees, and providing his expertise on various projects as needed.

Things are going great. Other than some minor frostbite, Ken loves life here. Summer arrives and the parking lot is full of potholes from the melting snow and ice. The unpaved parking lot is a problem for the few months each year that Mother Nature doesn't impose her wrath. Nome employees feel that once they make it to their workstation through the maze of craters from their car, it's a major accomplishment for the day. Obstacle course runners would feel they have had a good workout.

As a technology consultant, Ken is responsible for creating a more efficient plant while assisting on the day-to-day issues that arise. This is a great responsibility, requiring Ken to interface with many departments. He loves the challenge just as an Olympic contestant embraces the energy of the moment.

Ken is out in the plant working on a conveyor belt problem when a small group of men and women approach him. He is introduced to his new boss and plant manager Wilber, a Digitron ten-year veteran celebrating his recent homecoming from a three-month manager training assignment. As plant manager, Wilber is directly responsible for plant shipments and efficiency. He is taking over the helm from a past manager who let things run amuck.

"The plant is greatly behind both on shipments and quality standards," Wilber states. "I want this plant to be the pride of the Company."

Wilber is very cordial and explains he sets high goals for both himself and his team. In order to reduce product waste and catch up on shipments, Wilber wants Ken to extract all the frozen digits behind the plant that have fused to the tundra during last year's winter freeze before the next harsh winter arrives. Ken has noticed the thousands of digits during his plant tours and wonders how they came to rest in their current location.

"Wow, that's a big project," Ken thinks. "How is it possible to clean up all these digits before winter?"

"In order to accomplish this task, support from each department head in the plant is needed," Wilber states. "You will need their equipment and knowledge of working with digits in this climate to get this done. Without proper support, this goal will never be achieved."

Ken, with a look of bewilderment from both the assignment and the direction he is given, is left to himself as the group quickly departs to follow the hurried Wilber. "He must be off to spring a surprise on another unsuspecting soul," Ken thinks.

Ken starts to work with the department heads to get to know them and gain their support. As he works his way through the organization, he sees many different personality types—*Gluteus Maximizers, Ascendo Inabilituses, Corporate Players, Spin-Doctors, Corporate Ladders*, and the list goes on.

"What a group and what a mess," Ken thinks. "This makes a trip to Leavenworth look like a pleasure cruise! This is going to take some careful planning."

Ken believes a plan needs inscription to be worked properly, so he first states the objective and timeline to achieve the goal of extracting the digits. Next, he creates a rough outline of the steps to achieve this goal, the amount and type of support needed, and the effect on each department.

Ken presents his plan to each department manager, makes modifications as suggestions are discussed, and obtains their approval with full cooperation. He takes the finished plan, presents it to Wilber who gives it the thumbs up, and Ken starts off on his mission to have all the digits dug out of the frozen tundra.

"How in the heck did they get there to begin with?" Ken wonders.

Ken proceeds on his mission when he hits hard ice. Things come to a standstill and department cooperation becomes difficult. Everyone seems to have another agenda with torches from maintenance scarce, drills from engineering not available, and cutters from plant mechanics on loan to other departments. It seems no one wants any association with this delinquent project and Ken is left to pick up the pieces.

As the project starts to fall further and further behind, Ken is called into a meeting with a furious Wilber.

"It's imperative that this project is kept on track," Wilber barks. "All of the digits behind and to the side of the plant have to be extracted to help with plant shipments."

"The quantity of digits is now different than the original assignment," Ken thinks. "Now the digit extraction involves an area to the side of the plant in addition to the original area behind the plant. I am really confused. The numbers have greatly changed as well as the assignment."

At this meeting, Wilber has several of his staff members present: Oscar, Senior Director of Quality Control, and a *Gluteus Maximizer*; and Hilda, Director of Business Ethics, an *Ascendo Inabilitus*. Their purpose for attending this meeting is to support Wilber and his agenda. Realizing their importance at this meeting, both Hilda and Oscar go out of their way to play up to their boss. There is so much smooching going on, Ken has to be careful where he steps.

Oscar and Hilda start making accusations against Ken demanding to know why the project isn't further along. They couldn't have driven a larger bus into the room to throw Ken under. Ken feels like a flat cat on a Texas highway and has to regroup to maintain his composure.

"By the way, your main focus is to ensure all products are built and shipped safely," Wilber growls.

"You should have known this," snaps Hilda.

Ken couldn't be more stunned if a large shell landed nearby. Through this total change of assignment direction, Wilber divulges his hidden agenda. "Wilber and Co. are really playing a game," Ken thinks.

Wilber's true intent now surfaces. He wants to make Ken accountable for production output and quality control. This falls outside of Ken's job responsibility and Wilber knows it. By masking his original intent, Wilber was hoping to lead Ken to discovering what is expected of him. Wilber has to divulge his hidden agenda.

When the meeting ends, Ken is left to figure out how to get things back on track. He decides to prioritize the importance of Wilber's adapted mission, what parties are needed to assist in making this happen, and what the potential outcomes could be. Fortunately, Ken gained a tremendous amount of knowledge of plant inefficiencies in his first months of acclimation.

With a revised plan in hand, Ken meets with Wilber and emphasizes the level of authority needed to be successful. In addition, he indicates each department's cooperation and level of participation necessary for this new mission.

"I can't be the only one contributing to the project or it's doomed to failure," Ken intently states.

Wilber accepts Ken's plan and grants some decision authority.

"You will need my approval for any work line stoppage or overtime," Wilber firmly replies.

Ken also emphasizes all *Gluteus Maximizers* and *Ascendo Inabilituses* need to comply with the plan. He wants to avoid any internal conspiracies. The most important thing Ken obtains is Wilber's signature on the plan. He gains even greater public buy-in through an email announcement from Wilber.

Ken starts invoking his new authority by informing managers and workers of this new objective. He meets with each department and details their needed contribution, how the contribution will be measured, and the anticipated positive results for participating.

As each department pitches in to help, results start occurring. Shipments go out on time with almost no out of the box failures. Malcolm Baldridge—former Secretary of Commerce—would be proud. Ken is praised for getting this done. Even though others are vying to take credit, everyone knows who the real performer is behind the results. In addition, Ken is even able to get all the frozen digits dug out of the tundra before winter sets in. Wilber couldn't be prouder of what Ken has accomplished and is ready to give him a new assignment.

Identifying

This personality is difficult to identify, as their very nature is to obscure their intent. The best way to uncover *Hidden Agendas* is to observe and learn from others, as their experience will lend insight to this peronality's tracks. This slippery individual is cunning, conniving, and conceals their true intent as long as possible. Their hidden agenda is created solely to benefit themselves. In most cases, this agenda conflicts in part or whole with the corporate directives. Clear traits are:

- Asks for work to be done that falls outside of your typical job description and/or company mission
- Communicates verbally without any paper trail
- Describes delegated work vaguely without specific plans or a clearly defined expectation level
- Changes details of workload constantly and without explanation
- Focuses anger on those who don't discover *Hidden Agenda's* secret plan and successfully complete it

Interaction

As discussed above, this is a cunning personality who has a premeditated plan created for his or her benefit. They are on a mission, and anything or anyone who gets in the way of it will usually cause conflict.

If you have to work with or for a *Hidden Agenda,* it's best to document a plan—just as Ken did—and get their approval before heading down a path that may lead to conflict. One important thing for you to note is you should obtain their signature on any plan they agree on. This ensures when *Hidden Agendas* change their direction, you will have documentation of their original intent.

This personality may challenge you when working with or for them. If this occurs, it's best not to retaliate as they have thought out their course of action and have ample support to justify it. Regroup as Ken did and think through a plan that will get you out of the fire.

Partners/Political Alliances

Hidden Agendas will partner with those who can further their cause. As you can see above, Wilber had Oscar and Hilda participate in his game.

Sometimes, they will partner with other *Hidden Agenda* personalities. They want to compare their stories and outcomes. It's "fisherman's story time" to see who caught the dump-truck size fish.

This personality will steer clear of authority figures, including *Napoleons,* unless there is some synergy in their causes or they themselves are a *Napoleon* as well.

Long-term Effects

Hidden Agenda personalities love to play a game at another's expense. If you are aligned with this personality, then you are usually not the subject of their games. However, there will be times when you may be asked to participate in their plan. Over time this course of action will lead to isolation by your co-workers. You will probably find very few co-workers trusting and spending their time with you.

When you are the brunt of the agenda, then it's not very funny. Others, who are not in play at the time, observe from the sidelines and could perhaps be the next ball in play.

Eventually the word will get back to corporate on the games they are playing. *Hidden Agendas* will take a hard bounce, as their agenda doesn't match the corporate directive. The games will grind to a halt and there will be a change of monarchy as this personality and other game players will be scrambling for bleacher cover as the pink slips start falling. The game is over.

The only scenario where *Hidden Agendas* may benefit from corporate support is when the agenda they are concealing is one requested by upper management. This often puts them in a precarious position to choose career before friendship and ethics.

The Backstabber
(Taking Credit for Others' Work)

The Personality

In any environment there are individuals who perform with integrity, and those who manipulate the system and cheat. Just as a thief confronts their prey and raises their knife to take what they believe is theirs, the *Backstabber* raises their manipulative corporate pen to rob their business prey. This bottom feeder is present throughout the corporate world and lives off others naiveté. They focus on *carne la fresca* —"fresh meat" or the new hires—as their primary targets.

The Story

Ray is new to Digitron plant engineering after spending three years in the field service department. His tall, lean build along with a debonair look have the ladies turning their heads. A drive for self-improvement blazed the trail for his fresh engineering degree and has Ray exhilarated to make a difference in his new position.

Plant engineering's responsibility is to repair any faulty equipment and optimize existing systems. Many times this department works hand-in-hand with the new technology consultants to repair and optimize what the consultants recommend to fix or enhance.

Ray reports to his new position and is introduced to many new faces. During his first day on the job, Ray meets Frank who at first impression seems like a nice enough guy. Frank is stout in nature, balding, and has a slow, pleasant voice and demeanor. His graying hair and tanned, but wrinkled, face places Frank around fifty years of age.

Things seem to click between the two from the start and they hit it off as friends. They hang out at lunch together and discuss various subjects that include work, hobbies and interests. There are detailed discussions on where the good fishing spots are on Lake Tarmack and who makes the best bass fishing boat.

Frank spends time getting to know Ray and realizes he is quite a knowledge resource. He discovers that Ray's background in field service makes him very acquainted with how Digitron functions. It's a large corporate structure with many departments, functions, and corporate contacts, so the Corporate objectives can be confusing to many. Very few individuals figure this out early in the game as Ray seems to have done. Combine this knowledge with intelligence and an engineering degree: Ray has a lot to offer the department and Digitron.

A few months pass and the two are assigned to a production line project. The project involves redesign of the electrical system controlling high speed digit production stamping. The digits are stamped, shot out to cool, and then packaged. Faulty systems in the plants are causing overloads and digits are shot out at extreme pressure. Some digits are flung out of control through open production doors to the outside. Ray has heard of all of the digits frozen in the tundra at the Nome, Alaska plant and this control system problem helps explain how this happened.

The two start gathering facts so they can redesign the electrical system to remedy the problem. As the project progresses, Ray realizes Frank's contribution is lacking. Frank is supposed to research the "flux capacitor"—a key component that supplies high energy to the electrical system—and make recommendations on adjustments. This isn't done properly and Ray has to step in to complete the task.

"Frank talks a good game, but his actions don't back up his words," Ray thinks. "He's either lazy or doesn't have the background to do some of the work. I'll give him the benefit of the doubt. Let's see if I am judging too harshly."

The report is finished, and it's time to present their findings to management. During the presentation, Frank stands up and takes credit for guiding Ray through the process and solving the problem.

"Ray was my helper during this project," Frank states.

Ray can't believe what he's hearing.

"All this time I have helped Frank, backed him up when he didn't know things to keep his butt out of a sling, and now he's taking credit for my work?" he thinks.

Ray starts to rebut Frank's comments when the management team cuts him off in mid-sentence.

"It's our focus to learn about the report, not to referee contribution," a manager replies. The panel is happy with the findings and will document process changes for a retrofit policy to be communicated company-wide via an email.

Ray is extremely upset with his teammate. This guy is supposed to be his friend and he betrays him. Frank gives Ray a Cheshire grin, turns, and walks out of the room. His face shows he knows what he has done and is daring Ray to try to do something about it. Ray won't take this lying down or bending over.

Ray gathers up his notes and takes them to his boss Bert. After a hard knock on Bert's door, a large, stately man with a full head of gray hair and wrinkled face opens the door and greets him. Bert must be sixty years of age, but is still sharp as a tack—he's been around the block a few times and has witnessed just about every possible situation in business. Ray asks for a few minutes of his time and is welcomed to sit down and explain what's on his mind.

The office is cluttered with the spoils of many years of business. It stands as a museum of Bert's career. Awards, gifts, and collections of various artifacts amassed during Bert's business travels garnish every available inch of space. Ray settles in a soft, well-used leather chair that obviously wasn't furnished by Digitron. He starts to explain in detail what has happened, and how the information has been gathered to present the report.

"I had to pull Frank out of the fire several times during this project!" Ray exclaims.

Bert sits back with a look of deep thought.

"I know Frank from many years of working with him and have seen the tricks he likes to play," he thinks. "This issue does fit his MO. Ray is new, but I have observed him and even have several references on his past work performance and ethics. This doesn't appear to be something Ray created, but there is one sure way to find out."

"Since these issues seem to get worse unless dealt with promptly, I am going to have an independent, unbiased panel review the work of Frank and yourself," Bert exclaims as he looks up from deep thought at Ray. "I will let you know the time and place of the review."

Ray has a look of satisfaction on his face as he thanks Bert for his time, stands up, and carefully exits the museum without knocking anything over.

Bert makes some calls, sets up an independent panel to review the controversy, and phones Ray to let him know the meeting details. Then Bert walks over to Frank's cubicle to talk with him.

"Frank, there are some doubts on the statements you made during the digit stamping machine final report. I have asked an independent panel to review this issue. Please be available on Tuesday afternoon at 2:00 p.m. in the third floor conference room," Bert politely states.

Frank has a look of bewilderment that turns to panic as Bert walks off.

Tuesday arrives and Frank reports to the third floor conference room for the review session. Normally, this conference room has a large table surrounded by chairs to accommodate a group meeting. Now the room is arranged with several chairs facing a table where a panel of four men and women, already seated, are reviewing some paper work. Sunlight is peering through the drawn blinds and dust can be seen floating through its rays. There is an air of simplicity. All distractions have been removed from the room, and the mood is very somber. Ray is already there along with Bert, who is seated looking at the report.

"If everyone is here now, let's get started," one of the panel members says. "We are here to examine the work Frank and Ray performed to review the digit stamping machine problem. There is some controversy on contribution. Each of you will be asked a series of questions; the panel will review your answers and submit a report of our findings to Bert, your manager."

Ray is the first to be cross-examined. He answers the questions flawlessly and from the look on their faces, the panel is impressed. Frank's turn comes and he is asked several questions everyone can tell make him uncomfortable.

"Frank, we understand you were assigned the task of examining the 'flux capacitor,' making suggested calibrations, and then writing up a summary report," a female panel member states.

"Yes that's true," Frank sheepishly replies.

"Please explain how you gathered the information for the report," she continues.

Frank stammers around, scratches his head, and fidgets with his chin as he digs deep to come up with an explanation.

Everyone can tell he is welling up a wave of *Corporate Gumbo.*

"Well, I don't actually recall how I arrived at those conclusions," Frank admits. "It's been a few weeks now and I must have forgotten."

The results are less than impressive since major details are left out that should have been known had Frank done what is claimed. Frank is squirming as he fields these questions and it's clear he isn't telling the truth. With his fidgeting, stammering, and less-than-impressive response, the panel is convinced of who's telling the truth.

This reminds Bert of a story he once heard. "A complicated problem is solved with little explanation, except a miracle occurs and the correct answer is found. There is little evidence to support any of Frank's claims. How was this problem honestly resolved?" he thinks.

The panel thanks everyone for their attendance and reconvenes to discuss the situation.

"It's clear that Frank is playing a game to take credit for work he hasn't done," the panel chairman exclaims. "This isn't the first time such a thing has happened with Frank involved. What should we do about it?"

They decide to present their findings to Frank's manager, Bert, and let him take action.

Bert is called in to hear the panel's recommendation. He isn't the least bit surprised at what he hears and decides to take the panel's findings to Human Restraint—Human Resources. After pounding on the door for five minutes, a small woman unlocks the entry while rubbing her eyes. She appears to have been asleep and Bert's knocking disturbed her slumber.

He walks down a long hallway to meet with Sheila, his HR representative. As he knocks on the partially open door, he can see Sheila behind her desk working on a mountain of paperwork. She looks up from her toil and smiles as Bert enters the room.

"We need to talk about another Frank issue," Bert sternly remarks.

She puts down her work and listens as Bert explains the situation. Sheila is astounded at the findings.

"Come on," says Bert. "You have this on record twice before."

"Well, maybe we should wait and see if it happens again?" she suggests.

Bert threatens to go directly to the vice president of HR if something isn't done immediately. Sheila agrees she will take action. The normal course of action is to transfer the offender to another department or provide severance. Bert doesn't want to see anyone cut during these particularly hard financial times, so he encourages the transfer option.

"I will have to find an opening within another department and a willing manager to accept Frank," she comments.

Bert is satisfied the wheels are in motion to get something done about this situation, thanks Sheila, and returns to his office. Sheila lets out a sigh and shakes her head. She now has more work on her plate.

As she checks around the plant, openings seem to dry up as fast as Frank did when he was confronted with this issue. The word has gotten out about Frank. None of the managers want him on their team, so the only other option is a plant transfer.

Sheila researches other plant openings and the only one surfacing is at the Nome, Alaska plant. This looks like the only transfer option for Frank. She writes up her report and schedules a time to meet with Frank and Bert.

Frank walks into Sheila's office with a disgusted look on his face. He knows what is about to happen to him just as any guilty convict is about to be read their sentence. Bert is there as well to witness the event.

Sheila presents Frank the options of Nome or home.

"I will have to think about it," he replies.

The meeting ends quickly and Frank storms out. Bert and Sheila are left in a silent room.

Frank phones Sheila a few hours later and accepts the severance option. Word travels quickly that Frank is leaving Digitron. As he is packing up his belongings, Ray stops by to make a final request.

"Frank, will you remove your pen out of my back?" Ray says in a surly voice. "Some day you may need it again."

Identifying

Backstabbers are recognized when they steal or take credit for your work. Although not the most common personality in the workplace, one is always lurking to take advantage of a situation to get ahead. Key characteristics of the *Backstabber* are:

- Takes full credit for someone else's work
- Is manipulative and cunning
- Premeditates evil deeds
- Is not fully knowledgeable in their own job function
- Scrambles for a creative excuse when confronted about a wrong doing

Interaction

The key to avoiding conflict is to tackle the situation head on when you have been backstabbed. However, be prepared with all documentation and facts to support your cause. It's rare for a *Backstabber* to admit wrong actions, so documentation is critical.

Achieving a successful working partnership with a *Backstabber* is nearly impossible. Besides documentation, there is one other area to focus on for potential success: *keep upper management informed of the situation.* With upper management informed and your guard up, you can minimize conflict when working with this personality.

Partners/Political Alliances

Backstabbers will partner with whoever can help their cause. They know they are doing wrong and seek shelter from the fallout of their evil doings. Their actions are premeditated with a specific agenda to get ahead. Because of a *Backstabber's* behavior and intent, there will rarely be any consistency regarding specifically aligned personalities.

Long-term Effects

Backstabbers swim at the bottom of the corporate ladder. When caught, they squirm and plead innocence. They claim they either had no idea of the situation or are just a victim of circumstances. It can be difficult to catch them in the act of their undermining behavior.

The long-term outcome for many *Backstabbers* isn't pleasant. They usually end up being demoted or terminated from the company.

Should this personality be fortunate enough to keep their job after the stealing of another's work, the *Gossiper* will likely spread the word about them. In the end, after being flagged as a *Backstabber*, they will have to change their ways or move on to another corporation.

Klump: that fraud, that hack, that
no-talent! No sir!
This is the man behind Klump's work.
The real genius!
I give you Professor Buddy Love!

The Nutty Professor

The Spin-Doctor
(Tempering Bad News)

The Personality

A magician can make the obvious disappear right before your eyes. In a similar fashion, the *Spin-Doctor* can take bad news and make it disappear. How is this done? Sugarcoating bad news can turn what many feel is a total negative into an almost positive.

These individuals are the witch doctors of the corporate world. They stir their caldrons with magic brews to temper company negatives into potions that can hypnotize even the most astute. Any change in an organization can appear to be the work of a *Spin-Doctor*. Careful examination of the content and intent is needed to uncover any games.

The Story

Tammy has worked in sales for Digitron for five years and has excelled in everything she has touched. Her tall, professional posture along with a sharp mind and a head for business has Tammy at the top of the sales rankings. She fidgets in her cubicle, running her fingers through her long, dark brunette hair, frustrated with the news she has just received. Jerry —new in sales at Digitron, but a two-year sales veteran—is taking over her largest account based on a Company-wide restructuring. She feels betrayed and angry at the lack of Company appreciation for her well-being and past accomplishments.

After a few moments of thought, she realizes this isn't the first time she has seen this type of treatment. This happened many times with other employees in the Company. It's a tradition that lives on here and in many of the companies where her friends work. When a person is overachieving, a change is made to give those less fortunate an opportunity at the victor's expense.

It's the job of Jonathon, Tammy's boss, to deliver the news of the account transition. He is a large man with slumped shoulders and a sly look on his face. A ten-year veteran of Digitron and holder of six different titles since his hire date, Jonathon has seen Digitron from many perspectives. The Corporation has a master plan. Even though many employees don't see changes in their responsibilities as positive, it's his job to make them feel better about the adjustments. Jonathon takes this assignment willingly and loves to represent the Corporation. He is the master of delivering both good and bad news. With his skills, he could spin news that a freight train has derailed into a sheep ranch and deliver a story that lamb chops will be preheated and ready for dinner that evening.

Jonathon confidently walks over to Tammy—still in her cubicle—and attempts to soothe her anguish. He must carefully phrase his words to soften the impact of this change on Tammy while allowing her to see the positives.

"I certainly understand your frustration with this account transition, but look at the opportunities you have now with the extra time on your hands to focus on your other accounts," he comments. "I would love to have the good fortune of such an event to happen in my career."

"I must act like I gladly accept this change," she thinks.

Tammy's look of frustration shifts to one of acceptance, she acknowledges his comments, and thanks him for the astute observation.

"I look forward to the new opportunities in my other accounts that this change will afford me," Tammy says.

This gets Jonathon off her back. He feels satisfied this victim is well-indoctrinated and struts back to his office.

Tammy thinks more about what has happened to her. "Jonathon is like a polished politician making the bad news better and good news seem extraordinary." Tammy is convinced Jonathon is a *Spin-Doctor* at work. The *Doctor* has the ability to communicate the message being delivered in a way that either enhances the meaning or softens the blow.

This spin can be so intense that a twister could come through more slowly and have less impact than the *Spin-Doctor's* mastery. The web that's left tangles all those who are near, and they have to fight to regain composure. After further reflection, Tammy returns to reality. "Who would believe that whirlwind of a spin?"

Spin-Doctors remind her of the Warner Brothers cartoon character the Tasmanian Devil. He spins through the world taking bites out of things and people. She laughs at this image and knows "Taz" is often thought of in a positive light. However, *Spin-Doctors* are not perceived that way. They take bites out of people's egos, and most of the time this is realized after the *Spin-Doctor* has left their victim in a web of magic and confusion.

"Why do I have to give up success for someone else's opportunity?" she thinks. "I have worked hard to get to the top with no fluff, smooching, or the like. Putting the customer first and never over-promising has earned me all of my business. I still don't understand why this happened. Maybe Jerry is behind this. Was he smooching someone's patootie to get this account?"

Jerry is small in build, thin with wavy dark hair and a slick personality. Because the Company is tightening their financial belts, they feel Jerry—a rep with a lower compensation plan than Tammy—can generate additional revenues with a fresh perspective and perhaps the Company could save a few dollars on commissions.

Tammy decides she will approach Jonathon and confront him with her true thoughts on the matter. She walks over to his office and knocks on the partially open door. Jonathon is sitting behind his tidy desk when Tammy's knock wakes him from his afternoon slumber.

"I have been with this Company for over four years and haven't done anything to justify why Jerry is getting my account," she pleads. "I closed the account and have grown it to become Digitron's largest customer."

After rubbing his eyes, Jonathon hits the switch and turns on the spin.

"I understand, Tammy. I agree you have done an exceptional job. With that in mind, you are going to be given several other accounts. The re-organization is not only going to bring higher shareholder value, but also it's going to put more money in your pocket. And as we discussed, you will be able to spend less time working after hours."

Tammy begins to see Jonathon's point and is starting to feel better about the recent changes. After all, isn't a *Spin-Doctor's* job to turn a horrible issue into something you can live with, and perhaps welcome, as a change? It's like having a tornado demolish your entire house and then being thankful you can now save those bulldozer fees for the remodel you are considering. You almost have to slap yourself to come out of that "hypno-spin."

After further thought and a light slap, Tammy realizes she is being spun like a top.

"I don't see it that way at all, Jonathon," she replies. "I've worked my butt off for this account and made the Company and myself a lot of money."

"I know you have," states Jonathon. "Since you have done so well, don't you think it's time for someone else to reap the benefits of managing Digitron's largest account? I think you will agree it's the right thing to do, especially since you are the best team player we have."

He notices Tammy isn't buying into his spin. After all, *Spin-Doctors* have different levels of expertise and persuasiveness. There is the basic *Spin-Doctor* who comforts those who have to adapt to change. They can take a bad situation and neutralize it. They are like the "lieutenants of spin." A quote from the movie *Major Payne* comes to mind: "Let me show you a little trick that I learned to take your mind off the pain."

There are also the "majors of spin." These people can take a bad situation you are upset over and turn this into a positive event. You say, "Wow, this was a pretty good outcome," until someone rational walks by and gives you a good smack to wake you back to reality. It's a forest and tree issue: You can't see the forest for the trees. Details are hazy.

Lastly, you have the "generals of spin." These are full-fledged spin artists. They turn a horrible situation where massive change has occurred into a welcome state of affairs. They want you to say, "Thanks for taking me out of my complacent, great situation and putting me into this new untested environment where I can take the world by the tail and do great things." One needs to invest in some waders to get through this.

At that moment one of Jonathon's close colleagues, Frank, walks by. Frank is in upper management and is aware of the shifting of accounts Tammy and Jerry are going through.

"Frank," Jonathon asks. "Don't you think it's the right thing to do to switch accounts every couple of years so there is a fresh face working with the customer?"

Frank agrees and replies, "We don't want to let the account get stagnant. We can't afford not to switch reps."

Even with this spin/tag team approach, Tammy isn't convinced changing accounts is in the best interests of the customer, Digitron, Jerry, and most importantly herself. Somewhere in the back of her mind, Tammy feels like she should respond that she needs to go home and take a shower. The spin is running pretty thick.

Identifying

Even though it's necessary for managers to deliver bad news, it's how they do it that separates them from being a *Spin Doctor*. Managers who deliver news in a truthful, straightforward manner are just doing their job.

Encountering a *Spin-Doctor* is fairly common in the corporate world. They are the army of messengers sent out to temper bad news. It can be a very difficult task, but the *Spin-Doctor* fits the prescription. These are the physicians that intentionally transform the whole truth into a magic potion so that employees will feel better about the change.

To properly diagnose someone as a *Spin-Doctor*, look for the following symptoms:

- Acknowledges all change as positive
- Tends to be articulate
- Works hard to ensure others see the change from the corporate perspective
- Makes you feel like you are being sold a load of goods when the *Doctor* speaks
- Lacks substance to support what they say and do
- Endorses the corporate directive no matter how invalid it is

Interaction

Delving into the mind of a *Spin-Doctor* is putting your mental state of reasoning at risk. Trying to guess and second-guess the *Spin-Doctor's* agenda, and whether or not it's the entire truth you're hearing, may get you committed to the asylum.

By understanding the symptoms of a *Spin-Doctor* detailed above, you can find harmony. Traditionally, they like dedicated workers committed to the success of the company and themselves. Remember, they are the corporate disciples spreading the corporate gospel.

If you directly encounter a *Spin-Doctor*, it's best to be cordial. Then leave as quickly and quietly as possible. They may have ties high within the organization, and your reaction could determine your future in the company.

If it's necessary to proactively speak with a *Spin-Doctor* about a particular issue, tackle the issue head on and ask for the truth. Keep in mind you shouldn't come across too brashly. Being direct is the best route, but consider leading your conversation delicately. Ask open-ended questions about the news shared. Tammy may have had an easier time dealing with Jonathon's news if she would have tried to get the entire truth from him by suggesting she just wanted to understand the change.

A final thought in dealing with *Spin-Doctors* is to keep the important issues they are communicating in check. Search for the truth until there is understanding with the answer. Ultimately, you will have the most success working with this personality by having the ability to be adaptive and flexible with change. This will convey to a *Spin-Doctor* you are not only taking an interest in what is being shared, but also seeking to build stronger rapport in hopes the *Spin-Doctor* will be more honest in the future.

Partners/Political Alliances

Personality types *Spin-Doctors* gravitate towards are *Napoleons* and authority figures. These personality types have information they want to communicate to employees, and are looking for creative ways to deliver and support the news. The *Doctor* is ready for the assignment.

Long-term Effects

Over time, the effects of the *Spin-Doctor* are measured based on the reactions others have to the delivery of their news. As Jonathon tries to balance the "WIIFM" (what's in it for me) and what's best for the company, he could cause dissension among those who report directly to him. The team feels this way because the information isn't being delivered as the whole truth. This can make it difficult for the *Spin-Doctor* to gain trust and earn credibility from their employees.

If *Spin-Doctors* move into management and continue spinning, they run the risk of devaluing their leadership through diminished respect from their employees. The career results can be stagnation or possible replacement as their effectiveness for their talent has depreciated.

As you face a *Spin-Doctor*, the two biggest questions you will ask yourself are, "Where do I stand?" and, "Can I trust what I am being told?" If *Spin-Doctors* are to survive long-term, they should really look inside themselves and bring forth the complete truth. If *Spin-Doctors* can be honest with their employees and colleagues, the *Doctors'* careers will be built on integrity and they will be viewed as true leaders.

Ascendo Inabilitus
(Working at a Level of Incompetence)

The Personality

Everyone has a competence zone they operate in for both work and leisure. At times, the limits are pushed and an individual enters an area they are uncomfortable with and can't control. Just as any racecar driver becomes out of control when the environment overwhelms them, the corporate personality *Ascendo Inabilitus* is out of control in the business environment and works at a level of incompetence. As they ascend in their careers, they try to hide their incompetence by surrounding themselves with competent workers.

The Story

Roscoe is a newly promoted manager in Digitron's technical support branch. He isn't sure why he obtained the promotion, but he will take it and the money associated. It's a challenging job, but there's a good support staff that can make up for his lack of knowledge. It's not his fault he's over his head; it's the system—the Corporate system—he believes. A little smooching goes a long way, and it's a good thing he aligned himself with a *Napoleon*. This positioning helped him get the promotion with higher management's influence to make it happen.

Roscoe is a short, stout middle-aged man with a focus on climbing up the Corporate ladder. His thick, dark hair is graying on the edges because he spends countless nights worrying about the day's actions. He's in a new position with hardly a clue how to proceed.

After a few hours of pondering over the empire Roscoe inherited with this promotion, he decides to call a three-day meeting to get acquainted with the troops and lay down some ground rules. The staff should know what is expected of them and how this ship is going to be run. He has heard about several of his new employees, their abilities, and contemplates if they would challenge his authority once they figure out his lack of knowledge. He had better be prepared and rule with an iron fist to stifle any opposition. Roscoe works out a proposed agenda and notifies his employees of the meeting's date and time.

The meeting day arrives. Ten staff members who are spread around the country fly in to attend. Since the meetings start in the morning, the team travels the afternoon before to arrive and check into their hotel. After an attempted night's rest on lumpy mattresses, the group has a quick breakfast and reports to the conference room ready to learn from their newly appointed leader.

There are short, tall, lean, hefty, old and young members in the group. They come from all walks of life. Some have engineering backgrounds while others held more manual labor positions. There are degreed engineers who are almost over-qualified, while at the other extreme some work hard to keep up with the technology. Digit field support requires a variety of skills that include calibration, instrumentation, some high-level math, and a steady hand. Roscoe checks on each and every one's background prior to the meeting so he will have a better understanding of his staff.

Everyone finds a chair. Roscoe walks in with a proud, dignified look. He wants to make a good first impression and take control of such a distinguished group. The meeting starts with Roscoe introducing the department's goals and his expectations.

"I want this department to be the pride of the Company," Roscoe states. "There are other support organizations within the Company who enjoy executive favor and I want to change that. To do this, I need everyone to start reporting every minute of their time worked each day as you repair equipment and support customers."

Some staff members, including Ron, look around the room at the expressions on everyone's faces. Some have a look of awe at the amount of work they were just asked to do, while others have blank stares. "What a yawner! It's a good thing this isn't right after lunch when the food coma's normally set in," Ron thinks.

Ron is a tall, lean, handsome gentleman in his mid-thirties from the Midwest. His love for the outdoors, especially water sports, keeps him well-tanned. He has been with the company for six years and has seen many managers come and go. Some managers couldn't handle Digitron's requirements for high quality while others didn't like working in field service. Ron's first order of business is to observe Roscoe and find out what he knows about his new position and his employees' responsibilities.

"To satisfy my requirement for activity, each technical support engineer will make five service calls a day and ensure all customers order spare parts," Roscoe states.

A few words about the department and Ron quickly realizes Roscoe doesn't know the first thing about what his employees do. Each calibration job alone takes three hours, and the company reaps great profits from the service contracts. Meeting Roscoe's requirements would have each engineer working fifteen hours a day.

Ron loves his job. With his profit-sharing plan, he wants to see Digitron further expand its bottom line. He knows he can't challenge Roscoe's knowledge, so he has to behave himself. He will perform some background investigations, which will include what the true job description is for Roscoe's position. After all, shouldn't a teacher be qualified to teach their students? It's like the weakest link theory. A team is only as good as its least effective member. If that member is the leader, then the team is in big trouble because they will have a difficult time meeting Roscoe's and Digitron's objectives. With his void of knowledge, Roscoe's link appears to be made out of tin.

The day rolls on with the completion of Roscoe's and the Company's expectations. With such a boring lecture on material the group already knows, Roscoe's monotone voice after lunch puts everyone to sleep. "Why couldn't you just fax or email us this info instead of punishing us by requiring us to sit here and listen to this?" many are thinking.

There is a group dinner that evening at a nice restaurant, but they eat in the lower dining room to save money since Roscoe is cost-conscious. With Digitron's tight budget, employees aren't accustomed to eating "high on the hog," but

Roscoe goes overboard in his savings. The group gazes at the eloquent dining room and fine décor with all the tables set with fine china, linen tablecloths and napkins. Their glimpse ends quickly as they are escorted to the lower dining room to have their dinner. It wasn't in the cards to have linen this evening—only paper. After a few glasses of cheap wine—Mogen David would be insulted—Roscoe loosens up and starts chatting about his experiences. In an effort to connect with his team, he shares one of his major accomplishments from his last position. He details how, single-handedly, he implemented one of his ideas to increase management reporting at Digitron's Flatbush plant. He thought by keeping sharpened pencils at stations around the plant there wouldn't be any excuses for missed or delinquent reports. The group knows very well that all reports are done via computer email. "This guy is a real winner," the group thinks. "Roscoe either can't learn or doesn't pay attention to established systems and procedures. Either he is incompetent or just lazy."

After gnawing on some rubberized chicken substance, the dinner is finally over and the staff retires to their hotel at a quick gait before any more stories are shared. There are discussions between some of the group that go on over after-dinner drinks in the smoky hotel bar. Many can't believe Roscoe is their new boss. Not that any of them wanted the job, but Roscoe is so unqualified. They have to work with this incompetent boob and deal with all of his new policies?

Ron and some others discuss this further. They don't mind they have a new boss, but he should take some initiative to learn about his employees. He should understand their day-to-day responsibilities and issues. The group needs to find out if Roscoe can and will take that path. Is he capable of understanding their jobs? There is only one way to find out. One last sip of their nightcaps and everyone retires to their respective rooms for another long fight with the mattresses and overstuffed pillows before the meetings start again.

Wednesday is another fun-filled day of meetings with Roscoe. There are more discussions on plans, troubleshooting, issues, and the like. Roscoe reserves a part of the meeting for open discussion so the group can ask questions and propose items they want to be covered. He wants to hear some of their views.

"In order for you to fully appreciate our jobs, we propose you spend several days with a few members of the team on field rides within the next few weeks," Ron proposes. "This should answer most questions you may have about our job responsibilities."

"Roscoe will quickly learn the group's function and how he can assist," Ron thinks.

The group visualizes Roscoe riding with them. He will probably ask what a digit sprocket is and how much torque it needs. How much time will it take to educate him? Perhaps they can use the old left-handed monkey wrench trick on him—he will be looking for that for hours. (This could be fun since there is no such thing as left-handed monkey wrenches. Their design allows use with either hand.)

At first, Roscoe doesn't like the proposal. He feels threatened by this new staff. "Are they challenging me? Do they think they are better than me?" he ponders. Roscoe responds by letting the group know he will consider their proposal.

The day wears on, and then the next, and pretty soon it's time to return home. The group now knows what a person feels like after a good thrashing. In this case, all their marks are on the inside. The punishment isn't physical, just mental. It reminds some about a line from the movie *Trading Places:* "A true karate person only bruises on the inside." The group is all black and blue inside from this meeting.

Everyone says their goodbyes and heads for the airport. Some feel guilty, remember Roscoe's overcompensation for expenses, and comment perhaps they should be heading for the Greyhound station to save a few bucks and see the country. Did they receive a brainwashing also?

Ron loves the respect and praise the group gets from all departments within the company. He has to do something before this situation with Roscoe really gets out of hand.

"This is a great group and with the way things are going, the escape hatches will be blowing all over the place," he ponders. "People will flock to the competition or other companies to get out of this chamber of horrors. With turnover, the quality of the group will degrade and it's no telling what level of talent Roscoe would hire for replacements. Something has to be done quickly."

It's pride for his company that drives Ron to put a plan together on the flight home. He feels a manager should know his job, fight for the tools his employees need to be successful, and develop the group as needed to be a real asset to the company. To accomplish these goals, the manager has to ride with the employees and experience their day if he doesn't have any prior experience in this field. Also, he has to receive input from the group on their needs and understand that spending for the group is like an investment—if it's done in the right manner, it will reap multiple factors of return. And lastly, there has to be real goals put in place that meet the Corporate goals, but at the same time give those in the group some advancement in both their careers and their knowledge. The group has to maintain a positive attitude and enjoy their jobs to be truly successful.

Ron puts the plan in writing and the following day contacts several of his peers to review it. They suggest some changes. When it's complete, they agree it's a good plan. In order to make this work they need to lead Roscoe into taking action that will educate him on the staff he manages. He didn't accept the invitation to ride with some of the group, so they will present this plan to the director with whom they have a good relationship and actually reported to for a few months before Roscoe became the appointed games keeper.

In addition, Ron investigates the job description for Roscoe's position. It states the manager must have experience in field service to be able to manage a team effectively.

Ron is the designated presenter since it's his idea and he drafted the initial plan. He telephones the director, Mitch, and opens the conversation with some corporate goals the group wants to achieve. Mitch is a husky, balding man in his late fifties with a pleasant demeanor and an avid pipe smoker. Ron can hear Mitch biting on his unlit pipe as he takes in the details.

"Ron, this is a great aspiration. I'd love to see you and the others achieve all of the goals," Mitch enthusiastically comments.

Ron covers some of the obstacles he sees the group encountering. Roscoe doesn't understand the group's job function and is reluctant to find out firsthand. Ron notes that he doesn't expect Roscoe to know their jobs in detail, just understand the basics. That way when they request some support, or a new tool, Roscoe can make an intelligent, knowledgeable decision. Mitch agrees.

He covers the rest of the plan with Mitch and obtains full concurrence.

"I'll have a chat with Roscoe," Mitch states between pipe bites. "He should get to know the basics of his staff and there is only one way to do this. Patience is important and the group should give Roscoe a chance to succeed."

Ron agrees and the call ends.

A few weeks pass. Ron receives a call from Bruce, a co-worker in the southeast. "Roscoe is coming out to ride with me for two days next week," Bruce says.

"Wow, that's great," Ron replies.

Roscoe makes the journey to see Bruce in Georgia. It's a hot, sticky August day with a blazing sun. Roscoe isn't used to such heat and notices the bugs are the size of small birds. He has heard the mosquitoes are so aggressive, they have been known to carry off small children.

Roscoe meets Bruce and the two spend the day making service calls while Roscoe observes and learns. Bruce's knowledge is very extensive. Roscoe realizes he would have never known this had he not witnessed Bruce working in his own element. In addition, Roscoe learns more about his staff's job, their responsibilities, and some of the factors limiting their success in certain situations. He thanks Bruce for the experience and returns home to study this newfound knowledge like a boy who has just found a new bug or lizard.

He recalls what Bruce shared about being in the office.

"I have employees approaching me constantly with computer issues," Bruce comments. "Since I have a broad technical background, they believe I can help them with their laptops. I tell some of them to go to the sink, take some Ajax, and scrub the hard drive to remove any bugs or viruses. Some actually head to the break room to start this cleansing. Who can get any work done with those interruptions?"

Roscoe now understands why the team wants to work out of their homes. The quiet environment lends well to focusing on business, instead of being interrupted every two minutes when they are in the office.

The team requests the company pay for home phone lines and Internet access. Roscoe is determining if he wants to allow this. This is the *Micro Manager* coming out in him. Combine this with his *Ascendo Inabilitus* main personality, and the result qualifies Roscoe as a *Corporate Mutt*. Some employees are convinced they hear growling coming from his office.

After all, Roscoe did get this job from working closely with a *Napoleon*. He has to make sure he holds up his end of the bargain with management and watch closely over these people. Excessive spending and too many perks will spoil them. He wants them to earn their benefits.

Roscoe does very little with his new knowledge of his employees. He lets things just be as they are and studies what happens. His minimal experience, combined with the fact he's in over his head, is the cause for his inaction. Knowledge growth stagnates, trainings are cancelled, and expenses are cut to the bone. Some of the staff become fed up with what's happening and start leaving the company. Roscoe scrambles to replace them as they jump ship.

Then the *Napoleon* who sponsored Roscoe is dethroned. A shake-up at Corporate has the senior VP sending out a messenger to change rulers. With this tie eliminated, Roscoe is on thin ice. His department is turning into shambles and his protector is gone. Roscoe is in real deep "doodoo" and people better watch where they step.

Roscoe feels pressure from Corporate, and now more than ever from Mitch. His people are still leaving. Roscoe has to find a way to stop the hemorrhaging. It's too late—Roscoe doesn't take action soon enough.

In a few weeks, Mitch arrives and takes Roscoe out of the office. It's a long time before they return. In a few days, Roscoe is transferred to the digit-stacking department. Here he will not be mentally challenged, and there is a minimized risk of employee turnover since Roscoe is doing the stacking himself.

Identifying

In every corporation there are those who are promoted to a level of incompetence. They are barely functional in their new position and seek alliances with those who can offer support. With these individuals out of their comfort zone, you will rarely find them to be outspoken. You may notice they have a tendency to shy away from details. To uncover this personality, look for the following traits:

- Has been promoted to a position of incompetence
- Lacks the knowledge set to learn details of job
- Communicates with vagueness to conceal inadequacies
- Uses authority to stifle any threats to position
- Seeks out an authority figure's protection

Interaction

As mentioned above, *Ascendo Inbilitus* overcompensates for lack of knowledge with authoritative control. They respond in this manner only when there is a perceived threat or are directly challenged. Approach cautiously to avoid threatening this personality and causing any backlash. They may have strong ties to upper management as well.

When working for or with this personality, it's best for you to first observe them and then decide what course of action to take. Any suggestions or requests should be posed to them in a calm and rational manner. Position the request as a benefit to the company, not to the individual.

Ascendo Inabilituses are pinned in their positions due to their promotion to a level of incompetence. They can't divulge this inadequacy to their peers, employees, or management. Any disclosure of their shortcomings to these groups could result in reassessment of their current position.

If requests for assistance from *Ascendo Inabilitus* fall on deaf ears, don't directly challenge. Take note of the details of the request, the resources needed to accomplish, and the impact on the corporation for successful completion. Take this strategic plan to management for their support in motivating this personality.

Partners/Political Alliances

Ascendo Inabilituses will try partnering with *Napoleons*. If they can align themselves with a power figure, they can secure protection from exposure and challenges to their inadequacies. If this personality is unable to create this alliance, they will then gravitate toward anyone offering support and protection.

Ascendo Inabilituses will also try to align with those sympathetic to their cause and who won't be a threat to their own empire. *Gluteus Maximizers* will make a play towards an *Ascendo Inabilitus* to get in their good graces if there is power to be shared or administered.

They will also partner with their own kind to garner any knowledge that may help them keep their empire intact.

Long-term Effects

Ascendo Inabilitus is trying to carve out a mini-kingdom. As mentioned above, they try to partner with a *Napoleon* or other authority figure to help their cause. If there is a change in upper management, they are sent scrambling to find new support and cling to their little kingdom.

In the long run, the true abilities of *Ascendo Inabilitus* will be revealed. All those who work with and for this personality learn quickly that *Ascendo Inabilitus's* contribution is lacking. When company-focused management discovers this inadequate personality, coaching is offered for improved results. If this personality can't achieve refinement, then a change of position will occur.

Many times a modification in the corporate structure will naturally chase this personality away, as they can't stabilize in the changed environment. Any other personalities aligning with *Ascendo Inabilitus* in this little fiefdom will scramble for cover and new positions.

Does the Sheriff always ride in a taxi?

Yep, ever since he failed his driver's test.

Funny Farm

The Corporate Player
(Working with Blinders On)

The Personality

In the corporate world, rules are created as a guide to complement specific corporate goals and to maneuver through the corporate jungle. Thinking outside the box is sometimes necessary to achieve these objectives. Without this creativity we would still be traveling on horseback and scouring the woods for food, hunting with bow and arrows.

There are those who won't budge from their corporate tower and who look at the company rulebook with blinders on. They persist on their inflexible mission to uphold the corporation's stance on any subject, no matter what the impact on employees or customers. This individual is referred to as the *Corporate Player*.

The Story

Dave has worked in field support for Digitron for three years and loves his job. He is a stocky, short man, with a dark complexion, a thick beard, and he appears to be in his early fifties when in fact he is only forty years of age. His years spent in the corporate world have definitely taken a toll on his outward appearance. With short wavy hair and a to-the-point personality, Dave leaves a lasting impression on those who have encountered him.

He appreciates the Corporation's view on establishing guidelines, but feels flexibility is needed for some situations to be shaped into a win-win. To better help others, he wants to move into management, but has to be comfortable with a new position and won't manipulate his way up the food chain. His desire is to earn this position. With Digitron's growing market share and product line, he feels this can achieved within the next year.

He is assigned to work with Bob, a new transfer from Corporate, on a project involving redesign of a customer support system. Bob is a tall, thin, emaciated man whose frail posture has many wondering if he's like most in the corporate world who skip lunch to keep up with the daily grind. He fully supports the Company on any decisions made and feels nothing should be challenged. After all, the Company set the rule, so it should be followed and not questioned. Bob is looking forward to meeting Dave and hopes he shares the same sentiment.

The two men meet and find they have several things in common. One of them is they both love to hunt. One of Dave's old managers once told him that it was unfair to hunt with a gun unless he lay down and allowed an entire herd of deer to run over him first. If he were able to get up and shoot after that, then it would be a fair fight. Bob mentioned a picture he saw in a magazine where a deer was hugging a tree above the hunter sitting in a deer stand. They both laughed.

A few days after the project starts, the two run into a snag. Encroaching competition is increasing pressure on the sales department to provide creative solutions to their customers. One new customer, Zebratek, falls outside the current service policy guidelines. Even though they want onsite delivery of sprocket parts and are willing to pay for it, Corporate policy dictates they have to go to a repair facility. The customer is suggesting Digitron do the right thing and make necessary changes to the guidelines. These necessary changes make sense from a Corporate and customer standpoint to deliver the needed parts. The Company will receive additional revenues for parts, as well as new orders from a happy customer, should Digitron implement the new policy.

During some detailed discussions, Bob produces a hard copy of the Digitron Corporate policy mandating all customers obtain parts from repair facilities with no exceptions. He notes this policy should be followed to the letter.

Dave has worked with the sales team to sign Zebratek as a customer and knows the level of business they give Digitron. There are competitors vying to take business from Digitron, and in these challenging corporate times it's necessary to think outside the box.

After some research, Dave discovers none other than Wilber from the Nome, Alaska plant, drafted the policy. He has heard about Wilber, his many agendas, and that he was finally demoted to head janitor. Apparently Wilber wanted to play too many company games and Corporate caught wind of them. They promoted him to a position where his games would do no harm. He recalls hearing Wilber was fired from his new position because there wasn't a way to hide any of his agendas. Obviously, Wilber drafted this policy without any concern for the customer or others within the organization.

Bob demands this policy be adhered to. After all, everyone must follow the letter of the law.

"We may lose Zebratek over this. They're a customer we worked very hard to win, and they bring us a lot of good business," Dave points out.

"That's too bad," Bob replies.

Dave thinks more about this service issue. He isn't going to lose this customer over a rule that doesn't make sense. He drafts a proposal to show the value in delivering parts to this customer. Next, he highlights the associated cost for delivery and the additional business this customer provides each month.

He takes this information to his manager, Phil, and discusses these points with him. Bob is also present and holds firm on his Corporate stance that each rule should be followed.

"If these rules weren't important, they wouldn't have been written," Bob confidently states.

Phil reviews all the information and realizes this is a very important decision. He can't ignore a policy and violate Company rules while serving a customer. He has to obtain an exception to the rule.

Phil sends a priority email to Corporate explaining the situation. A meeting is called. Phil and Dave travel to attend. A panel comprised of representatives from field service, production, contracts, and Human Resources chairs the meeting. Moose Johnson, the Policy Director, is there to argue in favor of the existing policy.

Moose, a small man (obviously his parents misnamed him) is burly in nature and determined like a badger to defend his department. With a show of teeth, he is the first to speak. He reviews why policies are created and how they best serve all parties involved.

"This policy was created to keep costs within Corporate guidelines," he states. "Any violations are met with the harshest punishment."

Phil presents the customer's viewpoint.

"Is it right to ask one of our largest customers to drive to our parts repair facilities to obtain customer service?" he states.

Phil highlights driving distances, delivery times, expenses of both customer and Digitron, and the potential impact on Corporate sales.

"If we start delivery of parts to Zebratek and they continue purchasing at current levels, the net amount to Digitron is $600,000 per month," Phil states. "We can't afford to lose this customer over a policy that doesn't take remote customers into consideration."

The panel decides to write an exception to the policy for large, remote customers. Moose is furious and feels like his team abandoned him.

"This is not acceptable," he firmly states. "These policies can't be changed for an individual company. They were created to cover all companies."

The panel holds to their decision and Moose storms out of the room like a three-year-old that just lost one of his toys to another child.

Phil and Dave are given the go-ahead to present the revised policy to Zebratek and proceed with on-site customer service for sprocket parts. They are ecstatic and realize everyone wins with this decision.

When they return home, Dave makes a trip to see Zebratek to deliver the news. Zebratek is very pleased and continues their expanding relationship with Digitron.

Identifying

Recognizing a *Corporate Player* can be as easy as reading the corporate handbook—sometimes it's easily understood and other times it's as clear as mud. Some "in the box" traits are:

- Exhibits corporate tunnel vision—observing only what is written in the company rule book
- Never thinks outside the box
- Fights to maintain company perspective regardless of impact on internal or external customers
- Refuses to consider compromises that offer a better solution to the issue at hand
- Possibly has high ties in company to support mission

Interaction

The *Corporate Player* is on a mission to fully support corporate rules. Anyone who deviates from this rulebook enjoys an immediate and harsh response from this player. With such strict observance of company guidelines, it's best if you don't confront this personality head-on.

When you have to work with *Corporate Players*, calmly discuss the issues with them and back off when you see a fight could erupt. Heated discussions don't achieve any results except to raise your blood pressure. Gather facts that support any approach to increasing the win-win for your customer and company. Present these to your boss or authority figure to gain their support. This avoids conflict and obtains a desired end result that can become a corporate policy change. In the long run, the *Corporate Player* will adopt this new policy and support future issues that fall under it.

Partners/Political Alliances

The *Corporate Player* is on a mission to uphold company guidelines no matter what the impact on internal or external customers. If they hold firm to these beliefs in a situation that puts business at risk, they have few strategic partners. If they are doing this to work their way up in the company, then they will align with those who can help their cause.

Napoleons don't like *Corporate Players*. Since the *Napoleon* is a rogue manager, following the corporate way is a one hundred and eighty degree turn. *Corporate Players* restrict the flexibility the *Napoleon* has in interpreting corporate rules.

Corporate Players do become associated with *Gluteus Maximizers* and *Ascendus Inabilituses*. These personalities are like fish that attach themselves to those they see being in upper management's favor. If *Corporate Player* personalities are in that favor, then they will have to pry off others clinging to them for a free ride.

Long-term Effects

Corporate Players can make it to the top of an organization if they are in corporate favor, exhibit tact, and work ethically. Being manipulative and sneaky will result in creating enemies.

When there is any empire figurehead change, everyone will vie for new respect and authority. How the *Corporate Player* is viewed internally to the remaining department as well as externally to the new reigning monarchy will determine this personality's long-term residence and advancement.

What? Come on, don't look at me like I just
betrayed you.

No, betrayed implies an action.
You just stood there.

Miss Congeniality

GREAT TIE!
YOU'RE A GENIUS!!
GREAT IDEA!
GREAT HAIRCUT!
ARE YOU LOSING WEIGHT?
GOOD IDEA!
AWESOME PLAN!!
HA! YOU'RE SO FUNNY!
CAN I GET YOU SOME COFFEE?
WORLD'S BEST BOSS
GREAT IDEA!
BOSS

The Gluteus Maximizer
(Smooching for a Benefit)

The Personality

Most people don't play games to succeed in the corporate
world. They want to gain company merit through their own
hard work and results. Yet there are those who stoop to
smooch to get their benefits. They will flex to new lows to get
the job done in a way that creates deceptive values. Like a
cheat who wins a card game through false means, the *Gluteus
Maximizer* is cheating the corporate world to win the game
and gain some fringe benefit. These fast-dealing charlatans
deceive management while peers are outflanked by their
crafty, underhanded antics.

Independent thinking and morale are squelched due to this
personality's influence on management. No room is left for
creativity or the ability for anyone to get ahead through their
efforts as *Gluteus Maximizers* are looking out for "Numero
Uno": themselves. Opportunity for co-workers dries up like a
desert creek bed after a summer storm. It's management's
responsibility to recognize, address, and contain this personality so damage to the department and company is minimized.

The Story

Bill has worked in sales at Digitron for five years. He has
learned a tremendous amount during this tenure of half of his
sales career. Most of his learning and success can be credited
to his manager, Penny. She's not like some managers who
manage from their armchair—she's out in the trenches helping her team succeed.

It's Monday morning and Bill rubs the weekend's lack of
sleep out of his eyes. Still in his early thirties and a bachelor,
he plays as hard as he works. His 5' 10" frame and lean body
along with a great personality and warm smile have the ladies
ringing his phone constantly. He's introduced to a new sales
colleague, George, who seems a bit arrogant. Bill excuses the

arrogance as someone trying to create self-importance. He remembers first coming to Digitron and how others commented he was the same way. Things change, people adapt to their environment, and their true personality comes out. Some people are egotistical when they arrive to show others how highly they value their own abilities. Other departments perceive sales people as full of themselves, overpaid, and rarely putting in a full day at work. It's strange how perception can become some people's realities.

When eating lunch one day, Bill overhears two women from field service talking.

"How do you know when a salesperson isn't lying?" one says to the other.

"I don't know," the other replies.

"Their lips aren't moving!" the first woman exclaims.

The two women burst out laughing.

As Bill observes George over the next few weeks, he appears to have a peculiar air about him. George has an athletic body with wide shoulders and a large prominent chin. He has a thick head of dark, wavy hair, dresses for success, and exhibits a conceited attitude. George is confident he's going to succeed over everyone else, and wants everyone else to know it. He's always hanging around Penny and the director, Susan.

"What is this guy up to?" Bill thinks. "George has a wedding ring, so everyone assumes he's married. Is he out for something more?"

A week later, Bill is about to knock on Penny's door for her review of a new sales contract when he overhears George talking.

"I wish I could be as successful as you are," George proudly states. "Maybe some of your talent will rub off on me."

Through the open doorway, Bill sees the smooching position George is attempting to put the situation into. He can't believe what *gluteus maximizing* this guy is performing.

"The tone of his voice and his words are enough to make a person sick," Bill thinks. "Just do your job and leave the smooching to someone else. Let your performance speak for itself."

George is determined to become a manager—that's his dream. He has worked hard in sales, but it hasn't gotten him where he needs to be. He needs an extra edge, so he resorts to puckering up and kissing. George has become a smoocher and is an official *Gluteus Maximizer*. No smooching is too low to get what you want. This has become his motto and his MO.

Bill is disgusted with the whole situation. He wants everyone to get along in a professional environment. This "kissing" is nasty—a vile, putrid way of earning something you probably don't deserve. He has seen a lot of *Gluteus Maximizers* back at the Corporate office where they trip over themselves trying to impress the boss. Perhaps they can get a leg up so one could jockey over another and receive a promotion or a better raise.

He thinks about the *Gluteus Maximizers* and why they stand out. They love to be the center of attention and the teacher's pet. Always agreeing with their boss, it's their intent to make themselves and their boss look good at all times.

After a few weeks, Bill notices George is treating his coworkers poorly. Anyone who isn't in a position to help him is treated this way. He acts like this only when Penny, Susan, or any of the other managers aren't around. Bill has seen this before. *Gluteus Maximizers* play a game. Everyone is their buddy, and they are a team player in front of the boss. But, when the cat's away, everyone is dirt and treated like such. Bill remembers a joke from Saturday Night Live, something about an airline. "We treat you like dirt so you feel you have never left the ground." That's how George treats people—like dirt so they feel like they have never have been his friend.

Bill thought more of why *Gluteus Maximizers* even exist. From what he has seen, there are three main reasons.

- The first reason is *Gluteus Maximizers* are actually *Ascendo Inabilituses* in disguise. If they don't kiss to protect their lack of ability, then havoc invades their plastic bubble. They need protection, so they pucker up to get the boss to provide shelter.
- A second reason is lack of ambition. They could do the job, but choose to slack off. Here, they are similar to *Retired on the Job,* so they seek safe haven to make up for their lack of performance.
- The third reason is to get ahead. They want to install rungs on their peers' backs so they can climb up the corporate infrastructure, which makes them very similar to the *Corporate Ladder* personality. A little

kissing helps their careers, so they believe. This only works if the kissee accepts this level of buttering up and then obliges with favors and gratitude. Most employees are nauseated at the sight of such behavior.

The *Gluteus Maximizer* always has positive input and offers total agreement with Company policies. If there's a new process or sales plan Corporate is seeking input on, the *Gluteus Maximizer* is there to say, "Love it. Way to go. You're a genius."

If the process or plan doesn't fit with the field's needs, this personality supports and recommends it anyway.

The staff working for or with this individual are viewed as just bodies. "What can you do for me today?" is another *Gluteus Maximizer* motto. They are looking to promote their cause—themselves—and believe all others are there to make them look good. They want their managers to recognize their abilities and to offer them the highest reward possible.

Bill realizes what George is up to and how much damage he can cause. If something isn't done about George soon, he could ruin the department and its morale. While others work honestly and diligently to get rewards, this smoocher cuts in front of everyone to obtain benefits.

After consideration, Bill realizes the only way to stop this disease in its tracks is to ensure Penny, Susan, and other managers see the value of the entire department. When George becomes the center of attention and management stops seeing the team's value, this silver-tongued personality has succeeded.

Bill decides to take a diplomatic approach and create a plan to help remedy the situation. The result has to be a win for the Company and for all members of the team. He starts by listing the attributes of each member in the department and their contributions. Bill must remind Penny of the contributions of other department members.

After creating this documentation, he then schedules a meeting with Penny. Bill briskly walks over to her office, knocks on the door, and is invited in. He starts to explain his research when there is a knock on the door. It's George, ready to lay in another round of smooching.

"Not now George," Penny said. "I'm in a meeting."

George sulks off, realizing he didn't get his way.

Bill demonstrates the department's accomplishments without bragging or promoting himself in any way. He even illustrates the positive attributes of George. Penny agrees with Bill's assessment.

He voices his concern with the department's direction. Bill addresses the favoritism and staff's frustration. Bill doesn't want to cause trouble for George, but the department's needs have to be considered.

Penny hadn't realized the impact of George's antics on the team. She has noticed the decrease in morale and her lack of efficiency with George at her door most of the day. She admits this negative impact started occurring when George arrived.

Penny asks Bill for a solution to this dilemma.

"After all," she said, "You brought a problem to me. What solution do you recommend?"

Bill is ready for this one. He remembers some good advice from an old manager: "Don't bring in a problem without having a solution for it."

Bill explains to Penny that for team harmony, everyone should be treated equally—no favoritism.

"George has worked himself into a favored position not from his contribution, but from his smooching," he says. "While everyone else has put forth effort and produced, George has spent his time smooching to prove his worth. Expectations have to be properly set with George so he'll have a clear understanding of being a team player. This will require a private meeting between you and George."

Penny thanks Bill for his candidness and thinks about his comments. She spends the afternoon reflecting about the department and what changes have occurred in the past few months. Bill's right. Things have changed. She needs to have a meeting with George to cover the department rules again for clarity.

Penny summons George to her office. He waltzes in with his *Gluteus Maximizer* attitude when she cuts him off in short stride.

"George, we have to have a candid conversation," she says. "The department functions as a team. I haven't seen you interact with the employees in this way. There have been numerous reports of bad treatment and you are always trying to butter me up. Enough is enough. Only through hard work and results will anyone be recognized. Do I make myself clear?"

George acknowledges Penny's comments and without saying much leaves her office looking like a five-year-old that has just had his best Cracker Jack prize run over. His ego is squashed.

With George's kissing in check, the department takes on new life. Things return to normal. Bill sees it and so can Penny. The heartbeat's back, and people are enjoying their jobs again.

It's not long before George is in Penny's office again, this time asking for a transfer. He requests to be reassigned to payroll, where a new director was just promoted. Penny gladly authorizes the transfer and George is off to work on another group of victims.

Identifying

It won't take you long to identify a *Gluteus Maximizer*. Witnessing one who smooches for the benefit of getting ahead is easily recognizable. The attributes to look for are:

- Is overly supportive and praises inadequate work
- Has an attitude that doesn't seem genuine, especially when consulted for honest feedback
- Consistently supports select people in many public settings
- Is a "yes" person
- May brag to a peer group about a relationship with key company personnel
- Aligns only with personalities of power who possess decision-making capabilities

You will find *Gluteus Maximizers* networking with all levels of upper management in attempts to further their own careers.

Be aware there are *Gluteus Maximizers* who smooch for job protection. *Ascendo Inabilitus* and *Retired on the Job* can pose as this personality in order to gain shelter for their shortcomings. Indicators are inadequate work output, and lack of drive and direction in their positions.

The *Gluteus Maximizer* does have some value around the workplace. They typically put in a good day's work and will finish assignments in a timely manner. They traditionally can be counted on.

Interaction

Day-to-day involvement requires you to be aware and prepared for any and all types of smooching. From the subtle smooch (overly excited greetings) to the most extreme ("That's the most incredible sales report I've ever seen produced"), being prepared will keep your sanity and frustration in check. Be careful in balancing your involvement with the *Gluteus Maximizer*. Get too close and you may become or be labeled one. This can lead to dissension among your co-workers.

If you encounter a *Gluteus Maximizer* who smooches for job protection, approach with caution. Any threats to this personality's security can result in a venomous backlash that could include management support—on his side.

It's recommended to interact with this personality only when necessary. Approach them with an unemotional attitude. If you display an overly negative attitude towards this personality, you may find upper management isolating you from the ranks of career growth. Remember this personality will be working closely within a circle of influence, and if provoked, can cause you inter-office conflict by manipulating management.

Partners/Political Alliances

Gluteus Maximizers will partner with those who can help their cause for career growth. They want to climb higher on the corporate ladder so they can strike for a promotion when the iron is hot. Other peer personalities can be a threat and will be viewed as competition. They will make their best effort to de-rail one another or turn up the smooching to a new level.

Versions of this personality who smooch for protection will align themselves with anyone who can guarantee their job safety.

Management is the target of this personality. They want management's favors and rewards, so they focus their smooching there. Anyone who has valuable knowledge or power will be a key focus for all *Gluteus Maximizers* in the company. Additionally, this personality will spend time buttering up others in the department who they feel can contribute to all the above.

Long-term Effects

Gluteus Maximizers want to create a mini-kingdoms all their own. It's their protective self-created wall that shields their jobs and what they believe to be another opportunity to get ahead. If this self-delusion continues, *Gluteus Maximizers* will either alienate themselves from their peers or find themselves without any upper management support.

In today's corporate environment, being a team player is critical for success and career growth. Long-term *Gluteus Maximizers* will have limited growth unless they can recognize their own smooching and change their ways.

You can't respect someone who kisses
your ass. It just doesn't work.

Ferris Bueller's Day Off

F.A.D.
(Fluffy Administrative Delegator)

The Personality

The corporate world has many personality types. *F.A.D.* is one that many may have encountered, but not heard of. Some may confuse this personality with *Ascendo Inabilitus*, but don't be deceived: *F.A.D.* clearly shines as someone who has set their unique ways on how to do business. They differ from the *Ascendo Inabilitus* personality as someone who hasn't been promoted to a level of incompetence, but who chooses to function as they see fit. *F.A.D.* employs *fluff* to convey their feeble points, *administration* to recreate the wheel each time a task is performed or assigned, and *delegation* to attempt to solicit an army of workers to assist in the mountains of work surrounding this unique personality.

The Story

It's Tim's first day at the office and his manager, Doug, is escorting him around making introductions to various co-workers on the team. There's one person in particular, Bryan, who really stands out. Bryan, a senior sales executive, welcomes Tim to the team with open arms.

"Welcome aboard Tim," Bryan says. "I can't think of a better choice for a new hire. If there's anything I can do to help you be more successful, just let me know."

"Thanks," Tim replies. "Bryan seems like a real nice guy," Tim thinks.

As Tim gets acquainted with his co-workers, he hears stories about Bryan being a fluff sales person. The office gossip lands on Tim's ears telling him when Bryan speaks, his fluff is so thick all in the room have to seek higher ground. Each cube should have an oxygen supply so people will have backup air to breathe when Bryan is around since his words are so stifling, meaningless, and never-ending. There are also tales that Bryan loves administration and delegation, leading to a passion for processing paper where his work can be measured by the number of trees used to create reports. There are no off-the-shelf solutions when it comes to Bryan. He is seen frequently recreating Company presentations and standard correspondence.

Thousands of pieces of paper are used for the dozens of revisions necessary to arrive at Bryan's totally fluffy reports. It would make anyone cry at the thought of all that waste. Employees consider purchasing Weyerhaeuser or Georgia Pacific stock just on the basis of this *F.A.D.* The volume of paper products that Bryan chews through has to increase each of their bottom lines, so why not get in on some of the action?

The employees visualize a paper mill built adjacent to their building just for Bryan. After all, his cube is constantly overflowing with paper of all kinds. Expect no less than fifty different revisions of the same document. Scattered around are reports, surveys, and contracts. If it can be created, it can be found in Bryan's cube.

Another office rumor is Bryan lost one of his customers in the piles of wasted paper in his cube. The poor guy wandered in looking for Bryan and was caught in an avalanche of unstable reports. With all of this waste, employees who work with Bryan imagine trees have nightmares about him every night. Some day it will be their turn to become part of one of his fluffy reports.

"Well, enough of these warped thoughts," Tim comments to himself. He never likes to judge anyone on others' comments. He prefers to experience things for himself.

After his first few weeks on the job, Tim starts to settle into his position as an account executive. Upon observation of Bryan's brash attitude and authoritative behavior, Tim becomes very intrigued by how this differs from when they first met. He also observes Bryan interacting with other co-workers.

"What is it about my business you don't find important enough to handle my paperwork?" Bryan barks at Janie, one of the office support personnel.

"It's not my job to do your paperwork, Bryan," she replies in a firm yet professional manner.

"In my past jobs I had fifteen different secretaries who would help me whenever I needed anything. This is what I need to be successful!" Bryan barks back.

Tim notices this volley-like encounter and how it upsets Bryan. The *F.A.D.'s* head begins to glow like a sunset. Although Bryan does become increasingly upset, Tim recognizes how Janie's firmness squelches the situation and causes Bryan to retreat to his cube.

During a late lunch in the break room, Janie comes in to get some coffee. She notices Tim and sits down to chat with him. Tim comments he heard Bryan and Janie having a discussion earlier that day. Janie is exasperated.

"I have never worked with anyone like Bryan," she comments. "This guy believes everyone works for him and it's their job to serve his needs. I can't take this abuse any more so I reported him to Human Resources. They will be looking into it further. He treats me like a peasant woman. Bryan throws papers my way to be processed and has a complete lack of respect for what I may be working on at that moment. I feel as if Bryan believes I should be grateful to do his work. Hogwash! I won't put up with this."

She apologizes for dumping on Tim, and then returns to her cube to continue with her daily office responsibilities. Tim has now personally witnessed Bryan's passion for delegation.

Later that day Tim has an appointment to spend time in the field with Bryan, the savvy, smooth veteran. Tim is looking forward to this time with the self-appointed "best salesperson" at Digitron. This will afford him an opportunity to learn firsthand about the products and services offered and how to sell them. Tim has already spent time reviewing some of Digitron's many product brochures, and he wants to see how best to apply this knowledge so he can be successful.

It's time for the master to demonstrate his talents, so Bryan packs up his large stack of papers, loads up his dolly, picks up Tim, and they jump into Bryan's new BMW to head off to their first appointment.

"So how do you like it so far, Tim?" Bryan asks.

"It's great," Tim replies. "I want to tell you how much I appreciate you spending the time to help me."

"No problem, Tim," Bryan states proudly. "Just sit back and watch the master and you just might learn something."

As Bryan swerves between cars on the way to their appointment, Tim has to listen as Bryan discusses his past, detailing how successful he has been and how much money he has made.

"I've had a tough time uncovering opportunities in a few of my accounts," Bryan states. "But, don't fear, I'm on the verge of closing some really large opportunities."

Tim inquires about Digitron's products and services. After a fuzzy explanation from Bryan, Tim asks how he prepares for appointments.

"Glad you asked, Tim," states Bryan. "On nights before appointments, whether it's a first or second appointment, I'm always at the office at least until midnight working on documentation to present at my meetings."

"What kind of documentation, Bryan?"

"The kind I need to be successful," Bryan snaps. "I just finished a 45-page color presentation last night which demonstrates how to set up our products. The biggest problem was I found three different typing errors and had to reprint the entire presentation four times until I got it right."

Tim has a computer background and knows Digitron uses Microsoft PowerPoint for its presentations. He wonders why Bryan just didn't reprint the pages with errors instead of the entire report.

"There are forests being slaughtered just to service Bryan's ignorance. How many trees in the Amazon are going to be cut down just to replenish Bryan's paper printing extravaganza? This is way too much administration," Tim thinks.

They arrive at the appointment and Tim is eager to watch the self-acclaimed "master."

After greeting the customer, Tim notices Bryan's style of relationship building is similar to that of a used car salesman. Tim imagines a dog ready to run in to save the sale like in the movie *Used Cars*.

"Good to see you again, Mr. Jones," Bryan says to his customer with a wink and a smile. "Thanks for taking the time to meet with me and one of our new hires, Tim."

As the sales meeting commences, Tim notices that Bryan monopolizes 95% of the conversation by talking about a new product which Digitron is offering. Since Tim had reviewed that particular product brochure prior to leaving the office, he identifies the verbiage that Bryan's spewing as fluff. Although Tim is new to the Company, he has a few years of sales experience. He remembers a few things from his past training, including something about it being good to understand the customer's needs prior to discussing any potential products or services. Tim's co-workers used to call what Bryan is doing "show up and throw up" or "verbal vomit." Show up for an appointment, throw all this information on the table and at the customer, and see what sticks. It's like playing a food-throwing game with your business.

After Bryan speaks for nearly thirty minutes—hardly taking a breath between feather expulsions—Mr. Jones blindsides him by asking about new product features, benefits and pricing.

"Well, Bryan, I'm not convinced we really need this product, but why don't you tell me more about it and the pricing structure?"

Bryan immediately looks at Tim and says, "Why don't you go ahead and take this one?"

What makes matters worse is that Bryan is carrying a smile from ear to ear. Mr. Jones looks dazed and confused as to why the new hire, Tim, is supposed to answer a pricing question when he has been on the job for only a few days. This is Bryan's account and has been for more than a year now. Tim works his way through the pricing question as Bryan sits back looking dignified, analogous to anyone who has just deferred work onto someone else.

Concluding the meeting, Mr. Jones chooses not to buy the new product and tells Bryan it's not a good fit. Bryan doesn't give up and is still trying to push the product on the customer as Tim and Bryan are being rushed out the door.

"I really have to get to my next meeting, Bryan, but I will be in touch," Mr. Jones says as he shuts the door.

This is a classic example of the fluff and delegation traits of *F.A.D.* The fluff is flying as Bryan attempts to work his way through product descriptions and pricing. Unable to do so, he looks to dump the responsibilities onto Tim, who looks willing and ready to help *F.A.D.* out of a jam. The key here—if you accompany this personality—is to know the Company's products and services, because at any time they may shift the limelight to help field a question.

The next appointment is with a prospect. Here, Tim really has a chance to watch Bryan and his fluff shine.

As they walk up to the receptionist, Bryan with an ear-to-ear smile says to her, "Wow, you look really nice today. Did you just get your haircut?"

The receptionist looks up from her work and with a sneer responds, "Let me guess. You're in sales? Do you have an appointment?"

"Not exactly, but I know I have something your company needs to stay in business," Bryan replies. "Who can I meet with to discuss the products and services I have to offer?"

The sneer turns to disgust, as she has to listen to Bryan. The pretty face becomes wrinkled with a scowl looking straight into Bryan's eyes.

"You will have to call back and set an appointment," she responds.

Bryan finally takes notice of someone else beside himself and decides it would be best to call back later.

During the drive back to the office it's clear to Tim that Bryan is a *F.A.D.* Bryan is a legend in his own mind and he spews fluff whenever possible. This includes his Slick Willy communication tactics, the late nights he spends working on the reprinting of huge presentations, and the delegation of responsibilities to Tim for the pricing and product information. *F.A.D.* is written all over Bryan's face.

A few months pass and the branch sales manager pays a visit to Bryan. It seems he has produced only a fraction of his year-to-date quota, and it's time to make a pitching change. Tim overhears part of the conversation as Bryan follows the manager to his office. Thirty minutes later, Tim hears rustling noises. It sounds like Bryan is packing.

"What's up, Bryan?" Tim inquires.

"The Company is letting me go," Bryan replies sadly. "They don't know what they are missing out on, because I have so many accounts ready to close. There are five pending contracts for 2800 units waiting for legal to approve."

Bryan completes his packing and is escorted from the building.

That afternoon there is a sales meeting and the group is informed of Bryan's change of employee status. His year-to-date sales performance is shared and everyone's jaws drop in shock at the low number. No one knew it was that bad.

"You could sell more waiting at your desk for customers to phone in orders," some think.

Over the next few months, none of the accounts Bryan had positioned as real winners and ready to close ever amount to any sales. Nothing ever came of the 2800 pending units. Instead, stories are heard of competitors making great strides in Bryan's former territory. Digitron's rivals are fighting over the low hanging fruit as the Company is wading through Bryan's sales fiasco.

As new sales executives visit Bryan's former accounts, customer stories of horrid experiences and sales pitches practically made at gunpoint are shared. The Company is glad to be rid of such a sales deterrent, de-motivator, and liability.

Identifying

A *F.A.D.* can be a bit challenging to initially identify. Since they display all three characteristics (fluff, administration, and delegation) a person has to be on their toes to identify them. They have to be very observant of all of the personalities that make up this unique personality type. Their fluff may lead you to believe you are dealing with a *Spin-Doctor*. Their passion for administration can point you towards a *Micro Manager*. And delegation can be mistaken for the *Court Adviser* who loves authority without any responsibility. It's the three dominant traits—fluff, administration, and delegation—that separate F.A.D. from all others.

In addition, look for these traits:

- Exhibits passion for paperwork
- Frequently works late hours in the office processing paper
- Loves to recreate work for reports, correspondence, etc.
- Diverts standard questions during meetings to anyone who can help answer them
- Has a tendency to belittle co-workers
- Believes, "The world revolves around me!"
- Likes to dominate conversations

Interaction

Interacting with *F.A.D.* can be entertaining, challenging and frustrating all at the same time.   Challenging the fluff side is pointless. It's about as successful as gluing feathers to your body and attempting to fly. It's impossible.

The administration side tangles *F.A.D.* up in their work. As Tim saw, Bryan is slaughtering forests to get his work done. With some basic computer skills, Bryan could at least plow his way faster through all that paperwork and save a few trees.

The delegation part of *F.A.D.* can be strangling at best. The best way to interact is to stay away and escalate to management or Human Resources. Janie did this when Bryan pushed the limits by making her his personal secretary.

F.A.D. will push the limits as a child will with a parent. They are also convinced their way is the right way regardless of what's best for the customer or internal corporate structure. This makes it even more challenging to interact because it's difficult to tell where one stands.

When first meeting this personality, you will have an easy time relating and interacting with them. Their outgoing personality and friendliness will usually lead to sympathetic workers feeling an obligation to assist. Excuses are a common thread. This is like dealing with the *Spin-Doctor*. It's best to know the facts and be prepared for anything, because *F.A.D.* loves the element of surprise. By catching you off-guard they can usually snare the unaware into whatever may be needed at the moment.

F.A.D.'s indecisiveness makes it difficult for anyone to adjust to this personality. Peer level employees will constantly be jockeying for authority with them, making it difficult to avoid conflict.   If *F.A.D.* has higher authority over an employee and they don't report directly to them, it would be best to escalate the issues to management and let them wrestle in the trenches with the master of fluff.   Higher-level employees should be direct with *F.A.D.* This is the recommended approach to a successful working relationship.

As mentioned previously, *F.A.D.* will often test the boundaries to see what can and can't be pushed to the limit. Parental experience will be useful here. They will test all authority to uncover opportunities for leveraging existing relationships and increasing their strongholds. This personality attempts to erect an empire for delegation.

Partners/Political Alliances

Sympathetic personalities can't resist the need to help *F.A.D.* This personality identifies who may have authority over them or who could actually provide something of value to them.

Napoleons won't be aligned with *F.A.D.* Their lack of business focus and confused contribution doesn't provide much value to *Napoleon*. If the *Spin-Doctor* and *F.A.D.* get together, it's probably best stated by Rodney Dangerfield: "One is like water and the other like earth and together they make mud."

Long-term Effects

F.A.D.s' friendliness is the key to bonding, but their lack of tactfulness in recruiting support on their projects is what puts this personality in jeopardy of long-term survival in the corporate arena.

Also keep in mind the bonding will take place only with those whom *F.A.D.* believes will be able to provide value to their mission. Because they love to push boundary limits, eventually F.A.D. will burn their bridges or damage relationships by abusing their authority or the people who have helped along the way.

Long-term, the excuses will run out and both internal and external customers will see through the smoke screen. The combination of fluff, which most folks see as lip service and lack of follow-up, usually leads to *F.A.D.s* being on their way looking for another place of employment.

Exploiting Talents
(Using All Talents to Get Ahead)

The Personality

Most individuals strive to get ahead with their careers. Many do this on their own merits in a diligent and professional manner. But there are a select few who use *every* talent they have to win in the corporate arena. There's nothing they won't stoop to do. If this means flirting or perhaps even more, it's not beyond their means.

News travels fast within a corporation, and it seems gossip makes good internal headlines. As *Exploiting Talents* works their way through a corporation, rumors start to spread on just how they achieved this accomplishment. Talk of after-hours dinners and weekend getaways with high-level executives start to surface. It seems none of this can be substantiated, but given the situation and people involved, it's often adopted as the office truth. Many times *Exploiting Talents* are qualified employees who believe they need the extra edge to make the climb a little faster, and of course, higher.

The Story

Kimberly has just become the new receptionist at Digitron's southwest office. She is thrilled to have this people-person position and on her watch, no call will go unanswered. Anyone who walks through the lobby receives a beaming smile from her pretty face. Her long, curvaceous body and beautiful long brunette hair will help her on her mission to succeed in the corporate world. She will do her best to answer any question or find someone who can. Kimberly won't have it any other way, as she wants to go places in this Company and genuinely enjoys helping people.

In her pursuit for career advancement, Kimberly's first order of business is recognition for her talents by upper management. She has to use all of her resources in order to do this and will put together a well thought out plan of attack.

Within a few weeks of starting in this position, several office workers relentlessly pursue Kimberly. They are tripping over their tongues when they see her at the front desk. In fact, one co-worker was mistaken for an unmasked Jim Carrey after his tongue unfolded from his wide-open jaw. Kimberly is very selective and cautious about whom she dates, for every encounter must contribute to her professional goals. A few months later, she focuses on an executive assistant position that has recently become available. She wants to work her way up in the organization.

Kim is determined to get this position as she feels it's an important step towards management. Every time Leo, the Southwest Sales Senior Vice President, walks through the lobby, Kim makes a point of giving him a beaming smile. Even though he is a happily married man, Kim is confident her subtle flirting is softening him up to help her career.

A week later Kim interviews for the open assistant position and gets the job. Her skills, along with some well placed flirting with management, assures that she is the top candidate. She's on her way to success and will now learn and master what she can about this new position. She is content, but not fully satisfied.

Kim continues to use what talents she has and does whatever it takes to get recognized. She stays late, comes in early, works weekends, and volunteers for teams to get extra recognition. She networks with influential people and, of course, flirts when possible to give herself that extra advantage for career advancement.

After six months in this new role, an entry-level sales position opens. Kim's manager believes she is a great fit for the position with her bubbly smile, great personality, and hard work ethic. She has worked hard and deserves it. An informal interview process is performed and she accepts the newly offered position.

Both in her executive assistant and new sales role, Kim makes sure to keep her eye on the Senior VP. Actually, she makes sure his eye is on her. He is an elderly man and she isn't engaging in any sexual misconduct, just a woman's persuasion with a little harmless flirting. She wants to ensure she has the highest possible support for her career advancement. After all, her male peers will have a difficult time getting Leo to view them in this manner. This should give her a competitive advantage.

Kim works hard in her sales position, excelling beyond her peers. Some of her sales associates believe Kim's sales techniques are borderline ethically. She actually unbuttons her blouse a few extra buttons before making a sales call to keep her customers wanting to order more. Some of her peers are astonished. The customers seem to like it well enough, as Kim becomes the top performer.

Within a year, Kim is offered a sales manager position. Her performance, along with some extra positioning with management, has her climbing the Corporate ladder. She has done well at sales. Now she can lead a team to do the same. "There's no way I am going to unbutton my shirt for a sales call," some of the men on the team reply.

Kim takes over and does her best to increase sales. She's a very likable person and doesn't pose any hostile threat to management or other peers. She works her charm through her personality and achieves results. All it takes is a nice smile with some body language, and the most hostile meeting turns into putty in her hands. Management, her staff, and other workers practically run to get things done she requests. It doesn't hurt "big daddy" Leo is helping on the upper management side.

It's only a year before Kim is recognized for leading her team to the highest level of sales performance in Company history. Upper management applauds her. They love her cheery smile and positive attitude. She seems to be on her way to a great career.

After another very informal interview process, Kim is selected to become a sales director. She is on track to achieving her goals and nothing will stop her now. When she reports to her new position, she meets her new boss, Susan, who is the Vice President of Consumer Sales.

"Oh, no," thinks Kim. "Susan's a woman. My previous tactics may not work this time around."

Susan expects everyone to pull their weight and no *Gluteus Maximizing* is tolerated under her command. Kim is going to have to use her work skills to make the grade in her new position. She can almost smell the VP of Sales position.

There have been rumors circulating around the Company about Kim. She is a very pretty woman who is unmarried. Based on what co-workers have seen of her sales tactics with customers, a few rumors (true or not) are assumed to be accurate. The rumors claim she is sleeping her way to the top. There have been reports that when she was an assistant, she had an affair with her boss. Co-workers note she was promoted to the sales position rather quickly without any prior sales experience. Other rumors circulate about her sleeping with a vice president to obtain the director's job.

Co-workers don't care whether Kim is, or could be, fooling around on the job. They do care that she could be favored in a promotion over them with her powers of persuasion. Job performances have to be reviewed objectively as they relate to work ethic, drive and results. It's imperative everyone is measured on the same level against the same criteria. Looks or abilities outside of work shouldn't have any impact on the final outcome of job advancement.

Others are jealous of Kim's success because she has made it to director level in just a few short years while they have worked decades to achieve the same. Given Kim has climbed to this management level very quickly and so early in her career, this makes her the youngest among her peers. Many are angry to share their meeting with her and feel threatened someday she may become their boss. But that's not how Leo feels. "That bright smiling face is always welcome in a meeting," he thinks.

People never determined if the rumors about her affairs were really true. After a while it didn't matter. Kim is well situated in her director's position and is doing quite well. She is selected for some special projects and is praised on the results.

A few years pass and Kim finally meets the man of her dreams and marries. People ignore the old rumors and life is good at Digitron.

Kim has made her dream come true in record time. She is proud of herself and what she has accomplished. "Some think I accomplished this unethically. They'll have to get over it," she thinks. She has heard the rumors. Whether they are true or not people will have to decide for themselves. All that matters is she is happy and the Company is pleased with her performance.

Identifying

While most don't approve of behavior like this to get ahead, it happens in many corporations. Ignoring the fact doesn't make it go away. Being aware and cognizant of it is key.

Others watch this personality succeed in the workplace and few really see *Exploiting Talents* in full effect. These personalities excel in hiding their iniquities with subtle work accomplishments and casual flirting. You will have to monitor their activity very closely to truly identify them. The challenge is actually proving this personality is who they appear to be. To identify this personality, look for the following traits:

- Likes to flirt, particularly with upper management
- Projects professional image on the surface
- Ensures everyone notices them and their work achievements
- Can be hard working, but uses extra talents for an additional edge against competition

Even though a woman was discussed as the subject in this story, it could have easily been a man in a similar situation. Depending on the environment, as more and more women enter the workplace and excel to management positions, a man could play the same role as in the story for career manipulation.

The point here is to show how *Exploiting Talents* can manipulate more than their work skills to get ahead. The importance is it takes two to tango. If there's reciprocation on any level from the other party, then the flirter has won and is on their way to greater success.

Interaction

Working with *Exploiting Talents* isn't a difficult task. You will find this personality outgoing, pleasant, and very positive. The frustrating aspect of them is they continually focus on making themselves look good and want to be noticed.

In the right circumstance, they can be good team players. If the situation allows them to promote their talents in a team environment, they are 110% on board.

For a successful working relationship, don't challenge them directly. In most cases, this personality has ties high in the organization and will use that power to repel any threats. Without management backing and caution, approaching this personality could jeopardize your career.

In addition, consider handling the rumors about this personality with care. If word gets back to them you are involved in office gossip about them, this could result in repercussions you don't want to consider.

Partners/Political Alliances

Exploiting Talents gravitates towards any authority figures who can help their cause: success in the corporate world. These personalities include the *Napoleon* and the *Court Adviser* along with any personality having good favor with upper management —the *Spin-Doctor*, *Ascendo Inabilitus*, *Hidden Agenda*, *The Untouchables*, and the *Workaholic*. Depending on where *Exploiting Talents* are in their career will determine who they will partner with. Ultimately they will seek the highest level of power and authority available.

Long-term Effects

In the short term, *Exploiting Talents* may reach their career goals in record time. This rapid succession to power and authority will leave many co-workers feeling bypassed and unappreciated.

Continued questionable behavior exhibited by this personality provides them an edge to achieve their objectives. As in today's world where unthinkable corporate behavior is being uncovered, this personality will be discovered.

Like all corporate personalities, *Exploiting Talents* will align themselves with those who can help their cause. If the alignment is very dependent on their current and future success and something happens to their corporate sponsor, *Exploiting Talents* can be left hanging.

If they become a team player and are recognized for their own merits from work-related results, this personality will thrive without ethically related issues.

The Cover Up
(Camouflaging Job Existence)

The Personality

There's always an individual who wants to be recognized for doing their job, but many don't want to put the time and energy into performing it correctly. The reasons include laziness, lack of pride, and incompetence. These people are unqualified to occupy the positions they currently hold in the corporate world. They expend all energies to ensure they are viewed in a positive light and seek protection from an authority figure for the work they can't or don't do. Frequently they are part of a larger group called *The Untouchables*—explained in a later chapter.

Cover Ups defend their positions, job ethic, and the amount and quality of work produced. They are offended when anyone challenges their ethics or production and take steps to cover it up. They obscure the truth in their attempt to undermine any challenges. They obtain support from their authority figure to cover up any details used to incriminate them.

This personality is unique. Even though many question how any corporation can tolerate such individuals, they still exist. They are hidden in the shadows, protected by a ruler to support their kingdom and act as a body to rule. Without subjects, an empire is barren.

The Story

Rudy has moved into a new job and is excited to be working at Corporate headquarters. So many new faces and the career advancement potential have him running to his desk everyday. That's a feat for a large man like Rudy. His 6'6" frame and the fact he weighs in at 250 pounds have him winded even though Digitron HQ is located at a relatively low altitude. Co-workers witness his quick gait. The breeze leaves his short-cropped hair undisturbed. At the age of thirty, Rudy is driven to succeed in business and wants to start a family. His first mission is to find a wife.

Digitron headquarters is bustling with activity, especially with the recent closing of a government contract. Development is about to start on the Deep Space Digit to be used for the Mars Lander. This digit has to withstand the rigors of space and the harsh atmosphere of a distant planet. One of the engineers suggested he be allowed to take the prototype home to let his kids play with it. If it could withstand a week at his house, it could survive anything.

Early Tuesday morning Rudy meets Dan. Dan works in a support department and Rudy is pleased to meet another resource.

During the next few weeks, Rudy's work requires him to interact with Dan more and more to gather information and to collaborate on joint projects. They sit in different buildings on opposite sides of the Corporate campus, so Rudy either phones or emails Dan when he needs some assistance.

Rudy sends an urgent email to Dan late one morning asking for some information to assist a customer. After a few days with no reply, Rudy phones Dan several times trying to reach him. Dan finally answers his phone and Rudy explains his predicament. He writes off the lack of response to a busy Dan. Dan comments he doesn't know the answers to Rudy's questions, but he will do some research and respond.

Two days pass and Rudy is wondering why he hasn't heard from Dan. Rudy picks up the phone and calls Dan. He answers and doesn't seem to be himself. He fumbles his words for a moment and replies nervously, "I have your answers, Rudy." Dan's response seems real and accurate enough even though there is some verbal scrambling before he delivers the details to Rudy.

"There has never been a reason to doubt Dan and his information," Rudy thinks. "I will deliver these answers to my customer." After explaining the details to his customer, Rudy senses some of the facts seem incorrect. He thinks more about the content and says, "I've seen weirder things at Digitron. What about the giant digit mounted on the main administration building? What nut thought that would stand up to a good wind? It was airborne for three blocks before it hit the local Hyundai dealership. What a mess."

Rudy speaks with a co-worker and learns more about Dan. Other employees have had various experiences with Dan and comment they can't depend on him. He's inconsistent and his answers appear fabricated. Some co-workers won't rely on Dan as a resource.

The next day Rudy receives a call from Dan.

"Rudy, I have the answers to your questions," Dan comments.

"This is strange," Rudy thinks. "Dan provided the answers to me yesterday."

"I was confused when I gave you those answers yesterday," Dan replies.

"Now he has real answers today, when before they were fabricated?" Rudy contemplates. "How can I believe anything he tells me in the future? In fact, how can I count on him again?"

"Why didn't you give me the correct answers in the first place?" Rudy asks.

"When the resources were available I obtained the answers to your questions," Dan confidently replies.

"What the heck?" Rudy thinks. "Is this guy for real? How in the world can anyone function like this?"

Rudy has seen this personality type before. This is the *Cover Up* who is undependable and unreliable. They can be a nightmare to work with.

Cover Ups either can't or won't do their jobs in the manner needed. They spend their day providing "S.W.A.G. s" (Scientific Wild Ass Guesses). Rather than learning the information or establishing a process to gather it, they create answers so they appear knowledgeable. Accurate information is sketchy at best from these people.

Rudy asks himself, "How can these people be allowed to continue to function in this manner? How can the Corporation allow this? This is terrible. Horrible! Inconceivable!"

Rudy remembers Dan works in large support group. He has heard rumors this group lacks professionalism. This group has performance issues that include a lack of accuracy, timeliness, and responsiveness. There have been numerous complaints about them, but why hasn't something been done about it?

Rudy speaks with Beth, his boss. He shares the recent "Dan issue" and what he has heard of the group Dan works in.

"That group is known as *The Untouchables,*" Beth responds with a look of disgust. "It's a group with ties to a higher level of authority. This authority creates a force field around the group to protect them against all who challenge their performance."

Rudy is astonished. He slaps himself to make sure he's not having a bad dream.

"Beth, how should I handle working with Dan?"

"Not much can be done with Dan or the group," she replies. "I have tried before with little success."

Beth's experiences range from a lack of responsiveness to fabricated answers.

"The quality isn't there," she says.

Beth continues to explain there have been numerous emails sent to Dan that go unanswered. When she calls him to inquire why she hasn't received a response, Dan's excuse is he's working on it. Dan adds if she had a real emergency, she should call him directly in the first place. Rudy looks puzzled as she continues.

"It's pointless to deal with these people," she says. "They were created as an information channel for the Corporation. The assignments come from high in the Company and little can be done to challenge why the *Cover Up* is provided this authority with little accountability. Things are backwards here.

"If the world operated like this, daily life would be a total disaster. Imagine trying to take an airplane flight when the flight crew didn't feel like showing up and doing their job. Phone calls and pages would fall on deaf ears as they did as they pleased."

Beth has found success by working around these people.

"Don't go through a brick wall, go around it," is her motto. "Go directly to the information sources. Minimize the time spent and dependence on Dan.

"Spend time studying the organization to identify key personnel. Rudy, you are fortunate to work at Corporate headquarters," Beth continues. "You can walk over and meet these people. Imagine if you worked halfway across the country. How difficult would it be to accomplish a workaround under those conditions?"

Rudy takes Beth's advice and researches the organizational structure. He approaches this task in a similar fashion to having multiple contacts within his sales accounts. A diplomatic approach is used to form strong bonds with reliable information sources.

The importance of this approach is to minimize conflict with Dan and his organization *The Untouchables*. This group's purpose is to justify their existence and serve the Corporation. If others are bypassing their services, their value is diminished. The Company may question their need. Rudy has an appropriate quote come to mind from the movie *Fletch*: "Well, that's where we are in kind of a gray area. How gray? Charcoal."

Rudy forms good relationships with true information sources. Dan is used only when necessary. Rudy minimizes the pain he would endure interacting with this group.

Newcomers fall into the information trap and are provided vague, incomplete answers that get them into trouble with their customers. The word is out, but employees must listen carefully to get the memo.

Identifying

Not every organization has the pleasure of having a *Cover Up* on their staff. The larger the company, the more room these individuals have to hide. After seeing through their camouflage, identification is easy. They exhibit the following traits:

- Perform work they choose to do on their own schedule
- Let work pile up as they select priorities
- Have little training or skills for the position they support
- React with venomous response to any challenges to their work ethic or output
- Obtain sponsorship from authority figures to protect their existence

Interaction

The *Cover Up* is passionate about work ethic—or lack thereof. They resist challenge and fight to repel any intruders who question their conduct or job performance.

Conflict with these individuals can lead to authority figures imposing punishment on the attacker, when in fact the protected is guilty to begin with. Proceed with caution and recognize their position of power from authority figures. It's best to avoid them when possible and form alliances with reliable information sources.

When it's necessary to work with *Cover Ups,* you must realize they may be relaying diluted information. Confirm their responses with trusted sources.

Partners/Political Alliances

The *Cover Up* seeks the shelter authority figures can provide. Their lack of abilities is shadowed by a protective force field to prevent assault from those who seek accurate and timely information.

This personality will befriend *Ascendo Inabilitus* since they have similar personalities. Since both of these personalities lack the qualifications to perform their job correctly, they partner with one another to support their existence.

The *Cover Up* seeks to become a member of an *Untouchable* organization. Here they are free to roam with little fear of poaching. Poachers seek to bring down those who don't contribute to the corporate mission.

Long-term Effects

The *Cover Up*, as mentioned, seeks shelter for survival. In their minds, they truly believe they render a valuable service and see little wrong with their contribution.

Like *Ascendo Inabilituses*, *Cover Ups* find themselves exposed when their sponsored authority figure resigns, transfer's or is dethroned. This can also occur when there is a break up of *The Untouchable* organization. Outcomes are quite harsh for *Cover Ups* as they scramble to retain their job or join a new organization to inflict their vagueness on.

The Sour Puss
(Just Plain Grumpy)

The Personality

The current economic times don't make it any easier on the corporate world. Even the most positive personalities can turn glum when they read the latest stock market report. But, there are a select few, no matter what, who are grumpy all the time. It's a lasting effect a single event didn't cause because the grumpiness is more than just a mood.

This grumpiness usually is caused by several events in an individual's corporate career. Like a child who is shaped by their environment, the corporate environment affects the corporate worker. Having a hostile boss or an event that negatively impacts their corporate career can create the *Sour Puss*. They withdraw and extend their claws so the world will stay away. It's the angry animal in the corner growling when approached the *Sour Puss* eventually becomes unless someone makes it their mission to save this drowning individual.

The Story

Karen receives a new assignment to document digit alignment and needs additional information to complete her report. She is short and feisty, but doesn't let Company politics get in her way. Her shoulder length hair is kept in a simple hairstyle so no time is wasted and she can focus on work. She finds Dave, who has been with the Company for ten years, is the best source for this information.

"Not Dave!" she thinks. "I have to work with him? Dave always seems so angry at the world. Was this guy born this way or did the cat get his cornflakes one morning?"

Karen wonders why everything seems to agitate Dave. Nothing seems to be good enough for him. She recalls he likes to be left alone unless he initiates the conversation. He seems to voice his opinions in meetings with a negative tone. He loves to talk about what is wrong at Digitron and what the

Company owes him. Rarely will he provide solutions or suggestions to remedy a problem; Dave just gripes. He grumbles on, makes statements how nothing changes, and feels he is always on the business side of the Corporate punishment stick.

"What could have caused Dave to have such a sour attitude and wear such a heavy frown?" she thinks. "Perhaps he was just born grumpy. Maybe the doctor dropped him on his head or slapped the wrong end of the baby? It's possible he had a hard time growing up. But most likely, his attitude was further developed in the corporate world. Perhaps Dave was demoted, passed over for a promotion, or never received the raise he thought he deserved. He also could have had a hostile boss in the past that contributed to his grumpiness. It could have been a boss who was too demanding and was never satisfied with the work he turned in."

Karen decides, rather than jump right in and start talking to Dave about business, that she should empathize with Dave and learn more about him. Talking with him may help her understand why he's angry. This could help form a friendship. "How can I get Dave to open up?" she thinks. "Maybe I can state some examples of how things haven't gone my way in the past to see if he had any similar experiences." Working with Dave in this manner will make this much easier than dealing with an angry co-worker. In an attempt to create rapport with Dave, Karen walks over to his area around break time and invites him to the cafeteria for a coffee. Dave accepts, and the two stroll over to the lunchroom for a hot cup of java.

Karen initiates the conversation. "Dave, how do you like life at Digitron?" Immediately, Dave opens up and pours out his complaints and displeasures with how the Company is run.

"The executives don't seem to care about the employees— just their own stock options," Dave starts. He then focuses on how the business world treated him in a past position.

"I had this boss who wanted to review every proposal before it went to a customer," he continues. "Talk about micro management! It was almost like this guy loved to see his employees grovel to get something sent out.

"On Monday, I submit my work to my boss, John for review and sign off. He red lines the documents and hands them back to me for correction. I work hard to make these changes then resubmit them to him for final review. This review happens every time any customer documents need to be sent out. If on Wednesday of that same week another customer requests an identical proposal to the one approved on Monday, I change the customer's name and submit to John for review. I get the identical document John had approved on Monday, back with red ink all over it.

"This is nuts!" he said. "The dog is chasing his tail in circles. It's like being on the threshold of hell. Why can't this be a simple process? After all, the goal is to get accurate information to the customer in a timely manner, make sales, and possibly have some fun. This is a head-butting exercise in futility. Where is this going to lead except to drive me crazy?

"To remedy this situation, I had thoughts of hiding John's red pen or better yet breaking it in half. I once heard of a trim carpenter who had cut a moody tile man's sponge in half and the guy went ballistic. Throw in a unique situation and see what the rat does," he continues.

"I wonder if this is why Dave is so cranky around the office," Karen thinks. "There has to be more than this. So many of us have managers we have challenges with."

Dave continues his career autobiography. He is up for a sales manager promotion. He has worked hard in handling customer's needs and winning many new deals to help make the Company profitable. The time comes when the sales manager, John, is ready to retire. This red line kind of guy is ready for grandchildren and hobbies instead of playing teacher to his pupils.

The sales director, Mark, has to make some tough decisions. Since John is about to leave and Digitron is entering their busiest sales season, he has to find someone fast to fill his shoes to take over the reins. "Who is the best person to do this?" Dave comments. "Another sales person, Rick, who works all the time and has great rapport with John could also make a good replacement. He works closely with John and is always in his office complementing him on his management style. The smooching is sickening. And, after all, Rick knows the writing style John looks for and does turn out more work than anyone else. He closes quite a few sales and seems to have the heartbeat of the Company.

"After a long deliberation, Rick is the choice. He gets the promotion and I'm told 'Sorry. Maybe you will get the job next time.' This burns my toast. I'm more than angry. I've worked hard and this *Gluteus Maximizer* Rick is going to be my new boss."

"Throw another log on the hostility fire," Karen thinks.

A few more years in the corporate world dealing with policies that don't make sense and working with several *Ascendo Inabilituses* and more *Gluteus Maximizers* really fries Dave. He is officially a *Sour Puss*. Not to the point of physically hurting someone, but he is just fed up with policies and work that isn't productive. "Why can't this be easier?" he says to Karen. "Why don't the people who make these changes understand the real world instead of making these decisions in their Corporate campus bubble?"

As Dave continues, they both discover they have some common experiences. With Karen's empathy, Dave has a new found respect for her and some barriers have come down. By sharing his experiences and with Karen listening, he feels better about himself. This helps build some trust in Karen.

"Dave, thanks for sharing some of your job experiences," she says. "I have witnessed many situations like this. It's just not right, but it continues to happen. What can you do about it? Either you have to learn how to deal with it or move on."

Concluding their friendly discussion, Karen asks Dave for some help on a technical issue she is dealing with. "Would you please help me with some information I need for a report I'm working on?" she asks. "I understand you are the subject matter expert (SME) on this matter. Your expertise is needed."

Susan is able to gather all the information she needs for her report, and is off to put all the details together so the assignment can be completed. Dave feels he has made a friend and even though he is still grumpy toward others, he has a special grumpiness attitude towards Karen.

Identifying

The *Sour Puss* typically exists in every modern day corporation. The identification challenge is whether or not this personality in your workplace is truly a *Sour Puss* or someone just having a bad day. Key identifiers are:

- Sports a heavy set frown appears to be a permanent facial expression
- Is agitated by just about everyone and everything around work
- Complains about everything
- Thinks, "The company owes them many things."
- Is consistently irritated, even on payday

Differentiating between a *Sour Puss* and someone who's having a bad day shouldn't be a difficult task. Look for consistency in behavior and refer to the above traits. The identification process should be easy.

Interaction

Working with the *Sour Puss* is a fairly simple process. The first step is to make sure you have properly identified the person as a true *Sour Puss*. Secondly, once identified, initiate simple conversation with a clear understanding this personality could turn on you.

If you are able to engage in conversation, then you should try to understand why the person is so sour. Understanding is the key to working successfully with this personality. There are no guarantees. Some *Sour Pusses* are never able to put their grumpiness aside. If this is the case and you are not in a position to have to work with them, then stay clear unless they make attempts to engage you in their conversation. If the *Sour Puss* does invite you into their world, then as mentioned it's best to understand and then empathize. If you can do this, you should be able to find some common ground and help form a friendship.

On the other hand, if you take an aggressive, uncompassionate approach to either working or communicating with a *Sour Puss*, you may bite off more than you can chew. This aggressive approach will only lead to conflict, flaring tempers, and dissension in the office. It's not recommended to take the brute force approach.

Partners/Political Alliances

The *Sour Puss* seeks the company of a similar personality type. When at lunch or on a break, they seem to gather in groups and exchange their daily gripes about the company or their co-workers.

Most power figures such as the *Napoleon* don't like the *Sour Puss*. They want workers who are motivated and spend their time working instead of griping. Other aspiring figures such as the *Corporate Ladder*, the *Court Adviser*, *Exploiting Talents*, and *Gluteus Maximizer* will have no use for an employee who rants about their job and doesn't want to get work done. Since the *Sour Puss* actually gets in the way of their success, these personalities see the *Sour Puss* as a hindrance.

Long-term Effects

Continued grumpiness will affect both themselves and others. If *Sour Pusses* don't change their ways, they will find themselves without many friends or acquaintances. Frankly, no one enjoys being around constant grumpiness.

The long-term effects on one's self if the *Sour Puss* personality remains grumpy are isolation and continued self-aggravation. The corporate world is in constant flux. Those who don't embrace the changes with a positive attitude usually don't survive. No one says you have to be cheerful in the work place, but being agitated with others is a morale deterrent. This can leave you in position to be overlooked for a promotion or terminated due to a reduction in force. Having a positive attitude can take you far in your career.

Every day is worse than the day before.
So, every time you see me,
that's the worst day of my life...

Office Space

High Promise, No Delivery
(Setting Expectations Over Capabilities)

The Personality

Many times the best intentions exceed the capabilities for delivery of a commitment. There can be lack of understanding on what truly is required to make delivery. A change in opportunity may also redirect effort. The end result is a big surprise waiting for the requester, and the backlash can lead one beyond the point of return.

Understanding is required to avoid making commitments beyond company limits. An old saying, "The more you know, the less you realize you know" is applicable. The more someone knows of the process required to fulfill the commitment, then the more they will appreciate realistic timelines set to achieve the goal. Any changes to the timelines should be negotiated prior to final commitment.

Meet the corporate personality *High Promise, No Delivery*.

The Story

Stan is working with site development to decide where to build their new West Coast operations center. It's a taxing experience for this unhealthy, overweight chain smoker in his early sixties. After many arduous meetings and late nights in the think tank, Stan narrows down his choices to Moose Jaw, Alaska and Tijuana, Mexico. With each location having both pros and cons, the choice is a rather difficult one to make.

He recalls how his cousin Jerome rants and raves how incredible it is to work at the Nome, Alaska plant. "Long nights and shorts days," he tells Stan. "Putting in a full day's work equates to about four hours a day. The only drawbacks are the stressful outside work breaks. During my smoke breaks, I am basically playing night tag with the local grizzlies in hopes of enjoying some fresh air without becoming the bear's lunch."

Stan realizes the Mexico facilities are more cost effective due to lower costs of labor and construction. However, the drawback is he and his staff will be spending their time running with Montezuma's Revenge instead of running from bears. Concluding the difficult decision making process, it's decided due to operational costs, the Mexico location will best suit their business needs.

Three months later the 400,000 square foot Mexico plant is completed. This seems rather expeditious to build such a large building, but it's determined the short time to completion has something to do with the water. One sip of the *agua* is like rocket fuel. They workers know they have to get as much work done as possible before their next trip to the *baño*. With construction complete and all bathroom breaks under control, they are ready to begin manufacturing and shipping Digitron's products. After having done such a great job in building this plant in record time, Stan is asked to stay on as plant manager.

The first order is received from Barnum Bilson, the West Coast Director of Sales. This overbearing, fit individual telephones Stan.

"Stan, did you receive the order I faxed?" Barnum states in an anxious voice.

"Sure did, Barnum," Stan replies. "Great job, but my concern is the delivery timeline. How can 3,000,000 digits be delivered in thirty days? What were you thinking to make such a commitment?"

Barnum sidesteps Stan's question and responds angrily.

"Don't tell me you can't do it! Don't you know how much money this order is worth? The customer is expecting full shipment in a month. Find a way!"

Barnum slams the phone down and Stan is left listening to dial tone.

Stan thinks about selling an order that large. "That's a lot of digits. What in the world would anyone do with 3,000,000 digits?"

He has seen digits in both Company labs and in the field. Working in a plant is giving him his first hands-on experience with them. They are stamped, shot out of the press, and left to cool before being packaged. He has heard of an incident at the

Nome, Alaska plant where a grizzly bear wandered in through an open door and was hit by an ejected digit. A loud scream was heard and a brown flash was seen as the bear exited the plant. All that remained was the smell of burning hair. That bear has more hands-on digit experience than he does.

Stan knows digits are made in many colors, shapes and densities with military as well as commercial versions. The military versions are made somewhere in the southwest where security is so tight, plant personnel are driven to work in windowless vans. They don't even know where their own office is.

Stan immediately gets things moving at the plant and hopes they can find a way to speed up production. The current speeds of fifty units per hour aren't going to cut it. Hitting the thirty-day deadline is impossible.

"At this rate we can produce about 36,000 units for the month, so we will fall short by only 2,964,000 units," Stan ponders. "This should make the customer happy since we will just miss the mark by 98.8%".

"That's close enough for government work," he once heard someone say.

A few hours later, Stan receives another call from Barnum who is yelling even louder this time.

"How are things coming, Stan?" Barnum yells. "The customer is calling me by the hour to make sure we're keeping pace to reach the three million mark by month's end."

"I'm sorry, Barnum. Three million units within thirty days is impossible," Stan calmly replies. "You are going to have to be honest with your customer and let them know we can't make your promised delivery schedule."

"Impossible!" Barnum screams at the top of his lungs. "I never say no to my customers!"

"It's not a damn pacemaker, so take it easy!" Stan retorts.

"Digitron is going to close its doors if we don't get this order filled," Barnum comments. "I don't care what you have to do, but get it done," he says as the phone line goes dead.

Stan thinks about this guy Barnum. "Does he have a screw loose? What knucklehead promises a delivery date like this for an order this large? It's someone who doesn't have a clue what it takes to manufacture digits. Those things just don't grow on trees. It's like a fine wine; no digit is produced before its time."

Digit production requires mixing the correct combination of chemical goos. Once the correct mix for the specific digit type is achieved, the batter is injected into a high-pressure mold and then baked. A stamping machine stamps out the proper size and the digit is shot out to cool. Digits are then wrapped in a combination of badger fur and naugahyde wrapper for shipment. This special animal product mix creates a unique preserving process so digits are delivered at their freshest state. Even though these wrappers seal digit freshness, environmentalists are screaming because of the animal injustice.

With a limited set of options, he wants to be a man of integrity and do whatever he can to help the customer who has been misled by Barnum. He calls his cousin at the Nome, Alaska plant and asks if they are set up to manufacture and ship the latest Digitron model.

"Hello Jerome, it's Stan. I have a problem. One of our sales directors promised a customer delivery of three million digits in thirty days. He really over exaggerated this time. I must have told him a million times to keep his commitments within Company guidelines, but he never listens."

"That sounds awful," Jerome replies. "Let me see if we can do anything to assist. I'll call you as soon as I have an answer."

Thirty minutes later Stan's phone rings. It's Jerome with an answer.

"Stan, I have great news. Since we recently expanded our plant for additional production, we are able to double your output. We should be able to have nearly 72,000 units in the customer's hands by month's end."

Stan knows it's hopeless to meet the three million mark, but feels a partial delivery is better than nothing.

The promised delivery date is days away and Barnum continues his call blitz to Stan looking for a solution. Stan receives a call from the West Coast vice president of Digitron sales. He informs Stan to stop production and informs him they have lost the order. Barnum has not kept his customer apprised of the progress and shouldn't have made such an extremely large delivery commitment to begin with.

Digitron upper management finds out about Barnum's *High Promise, No Delivery* and Human Resources is asked to inform Barnum his desk is being permanently relocated off Company premises. His parting gifts are his walking papers and freshly bottled tap water shipped directly from Stan's plant. You can run but you can't hide once you have a sip of this going away present.

Identifying

You will find identifying *High Promise, No Delivery* very easy. The key elements to this individual are:

- Glows with intensity levels higher than normal
- Sets unrealistic and unobtainable timelines
- Is a smooth talker for self-gratification
- Lacks knowledge of commitment fulfillment
- Blames other for mistakes
- Is consistently the target of customer complaints

Your experiences and the above key elements will make it easy for you to identify the *High Promise, No Delivery* personality. The most common business position associated with this personality type is the sales person. In a sales environment, the single identifying characteristic across all *High Promise, No Delivery* personalities is the setting of unrealistic expectations to win business or the sale.

However, you may encounter them in any department where commitments are necessary. Everyone is disappointed when a task is over-committed and under-delivered.

Interaction

High Promise, No Delivery personalities have a tendency to push their commitments and blame onto others. This personality will leave the burden of their promise on your plate.

You should be calm, direct, and avoid feeding off of their intense energy. It's rare you will be able to talk them down from their emotional high, but being calm will help the situation greatly. Should they respond to your behavior, perhaps they will calm down and be able to discuss the situation rationally.

Partners/Political Alliances

The *High Promise, No Delivery* personality works best with a *Napoleon*. The directness and assertiveness administered by this authority figure will keep their commitment realistic. The mixing of the two will create a successful working relationship. *Napoleons* give direction and set specific boundaries which guide *High Promise, No Delivery* into a more concise plan to work.

The high intensity levels of this personality severely limit alliances with other personalities.

Long-term Effects

The actions of this personality cause customer dissatisfaction and co-worker dissension. Just as Gekko in the movie *Wall Street* said, "All good things must come to an end," with this type behavior *High Promise, No Delivery* is on a crash course to end their career.

The remedy for *High Promise, No Delivery* is to help them find a way to set realistic expectations that are attainable. Managing this process needs to be accomplished by maintaining controlled emotions.

Winning business with lies and misinformation only hurts the integrity of your company, and can scar your career for life.

My word is like oak.

Jerry Maguire

The Best of Breed
(Ensuring to be at the Head of the Pack)

The Personality

Fear of being outclassed has many managers looking over their shoulders at their team members: their direct reports. It's their belief if their employees excel and are recognized for their abilities, then this may cast a shadow of doubt on the manager. The corporation may question their worthiness and contribution. Just as in professional sports, the coach is often viewed as a figurehead and not directly responsible for success. Likewise, the *Best of Breed* managers in fact view themselves as expendable if their team surpasses their manager's own abilities. "Why not replace the manager with such a successful employee?" races through their mind.

Although very obvious, it never occurs to the manager that hiring competent, successful employees who achieve great things is a direct reflection on the manager. Like a proud teacher whose students are very successful because of his finer guidance, the manager should consider a similar track.

The Story

Marty has just been promoted to field service manager for the southeast office of Digitron. He is very proud of this accomplishment having been the top field service engineer (FSE) for four years straight. Marty's internal drive has him at the top of his class and working hard day and night to polish his skills for improvement. All of the other FSEs are envious that Marty has been promoted.

This 5'10", athletically built thirty-something-man is ready to get the feel for his new position and start taking hold of the reins. He has attended several weeks of manager training and knows the position he will manage inside and out since he has performed the job for years.

Marty remembers as a field service engineer how difficult it is keeping the customers happy. He recalls one customer in particular who is a real challenge—Krusty Wilson. Krusty is a crotchety old guy who is very finicky and never satisfied. He wants everything done his way and his extreme requests exceed the support contract he has with Digitron. Marty has to realign all the sprockets on Krusty's digits each time he visits. Even though this isn't part of the standard maintenance, Marty takes care of it so he won't have to listen to a half-hour of squawking and griping from the elderly fellow.

The customers all know Marty from his continuous service calls and are very happy he has received this promotion. The current territory is expanding due to increased demand for digit support and an additional support team is needed to handle the growth. It's time for Marty to hire his team of field service engineers so he will have a staff to manage. He feels it will be best to ensure there are no threats to his new role so he needs to hire strategically. He can't have a hotshot FSE come in and endanger his new position. "How would it look with someone excelling under me?" he mulls over. With job security being important to Marty, he doesn't even like thinking about that scenario.

Marty receives over a hundred resumes and reviews them, pondering who could and should be candidates. He has to hire five FSEs and wants this to be a good decision for himself and the Company. Marty narrows down the list to fifteen candidates to interview.

He will interview five candidates per day and wants to have decisions made on whom to hire by the end of the week, so he starts the interviewing process early Monday morning. Being new in his management position, Marty decides to conduct the interviews himself and make all decisions. How can any ruler govern an empty empire? He wants to get his department staffed as soon as possible.

Monday morning arrives and the first interviewee is there at 8:00 a.m. sharp. Marty escorts her to his office for the interview. During the interview, Marty discovers the candidate has more knowledge than her resume reflects. He immediately visualizes a threat sitting before him.

"This woman has a successful history in field service and would bring a lot of value to Digitron," he thinks. "Her service rating scores are outstanding—even higher than mine are. If I hire her, she may have my job in no time. She may be too good to work here."

Marty is worried she may have too much talent and could threaten his kingdom. "What if she does a better job than I did as an FSE? What if people view her as someone who should be the manager instead of me?" he panics. This could jeopardize his empire before the concrete has fully set up.

The interviews continue with some candidates "no showing" the event. In one interview, Marty almost slips into a coma listening to the candidate babble on. The conversation is so dry Marty has cottonmouth. It reminds him of Jim Carrey trying to take his medicine in the movie *Me, Myself and Irene*. Jim's mouth is white with dryness as he desperately tries to wash down his pills.

By the close of business on Wednesday, Marty has interviewed fifteen candidates in hopes of finding five good ones. He has to call a few more in to replace the three that didn't show for their scheduled interviews.

After reviewing all candidates, Marty's goal is to narrow down the search to six finalists for the five open positions. Just like the first woman he interviewed, there are five more candidates who stand out with great qualifications and would make excellent FSEs.

"Hmmm," thinks Marty. "This can't happen this way. These top candidates could really cause problems for me. What if they want my job? One of them even mentioned during the interview they want to make a quick move into management. I have to make a decision on who to hire so the team can start training."

Marty finally makes offers to five of the fifteen candidates. It takes careful consideration and evaluation, but he opts to hire the mediocre candidates while letting more qualified ones go. He doesn't share this information with anyone as he thinks it could cost him his job.

He expresses his condolences to the candidates who don't make the cut and wishes them the best in their job search. The five new candidates accept their offers and are anxiously awaiting their start date in two weeks. They all have ambitious attitudes, determined faces, and are ready to make a difference.

The first thing on the agenda is to train the five new FSEs for field service duty at Digitron. Things are done at a high standard at this company, so the lot will go through a three-week training course before being turned loose in the field.

The technical trainer conducts a class comprised of Marty's group along with other FSEs from across the country. After their first day in class, the trainer is exhausted and extremely frustrated by the skill set—or lack of—in Marty's new group. What little hair he had prior the course is now gone in a few hours of pure mentor punishment.

Marty is sitting at his desk, pondering how to keep himself out of trouble for hiring substandard employees. He is worried if anyone suspects his *Best of Breed* approach to management. Suddenly the phone rings and wakes Marty from his stupor. It's the trainer who begins to give Marty a verbal lashing.

"Where did you find these people?" the instructor demands. Before Marty can respond, the instructor continues. "They don't have the basic skills to be in my class and they seem more interested in causing distractions with the other attendees." It turns out one of Marty's new hires decided to put a whoopee cushion on another trainee's seat. The sound made once the cushion was sat on sent the class into an uproar and caused nearly thirty minutes of distraction.

Marty profusely apologizes for his team's behavior, commits to having a discussion with the newbies about this, but sidesteps the qualification comment and refocuses the discussion.

"I would really appreciate if you could adjust the training so we can get them up to speed as quickly as possible," Marty replies.

After hearing Marty's feedback, the instructor emphasizes to Marty he will have a challenge developing the skills of some of them. "They don't understand basic technical information and these distractions are intolerable. You need to talk with them about this," he says. Marty thanks the instructor for his call and hangs up the phone.

The next day, Marty contacts each of the troubled new hires and lays down the law for behavior. This seems to straighten things out for the week. The group scrapes by, graduates, and is working in the field.

A few months pass and Marty starts receiving calls from external customers. One complains that Jeff doesn't do a thorough job when he's on site. It seems when Jeff completes his work he leaves parts lying around, and a few of his tools behind as some sort of customer gift. "I'm not paying any shipping charges to get these tools back to you," the angry customer says.

Another complains about Bill and how he is always in a hurry. "Bill comes in, throws down his tools and breaks a cabinet. There is a flurry of flying parts, he finishes the repair, and is out the door before anyone can ask him what was wrong and what did he do to fix the problem," another customer complains. The list of complaints goes on and on.

Marty feels like the complaint desk of the Better Business Bureau. The calls keep coming and start to affect Marty's performance and well being. He can barely get his job done with fielding so many calls and handling complaints. He talks to each respective FSE as complaints come in about them, and things improve only slightly.

Sam, a Digitron salesperson, is getting complaints as well. He handles a lot of the same accounts and customers are continuously voicing their concerns to him. Sam becomes very upset and calls Marty to let him know his team is sucking pond water. Sam has worked hard to win these customers and now these new FSEs are washing all that work down the drain in a matter of weeks. Something has to be done about this.

Knowing that trainers have a baseline understanding of students' abilities and behavior, Sam talks to the FSE trainer that attempted to educate Marty's group. The trainer has no qualms about being candid on the team's knowledge and personalities. He provides Sam with an earful of his interesting experience with the group.

Sam takes this information and compares the quality of FSEs Marty has hired to the other FSE group run by Tina. The groups aren't even close. A comparison that comes to mind is like the local football team, the Mud Hens, trying to win a game against a pro team. Tina runs a pro team, while Marty manages the Mud Hens who could hardly win a game if they played themselves.

Tina's group runs like a Swiss clock while Marty's is as efficient as a wood-fired space shuttle.

This was actually a question on one of Sam's tests in college—how much wood is necessary to power a space shuttle to the moon. It seems the fuel requirement to propel it to the moon would strip the earth of all wood. The mass of the container needed to store this fuel would upset the gravitational force of the moon, so why bother? Sam didn't get an A on that test. "Enough of these memories of college," Sam thinks.

Sam's research shows customers love the work of Tina's team. She hears nothing but compliments on her people. Tina has hired excellent people who want to be at work and care about their personal performance.

After hearing the feedback from the trainer and performing the research on Tina's team, Sam immediately phones Marty and emphasizes these customer service issues had better be fixed quickly or customers will start to take their business to Digitron's competitors. "I suggest you speak with Tina to discuss why her team is so successful," he says.

Marty welcomes the suggestion and decides to talk with Tina about things. He calls her and schedules a time for them to meet and discuss how to make his team successful. "I have some free time right now if you want to come over to my office," she says to Marty.

Marty makes the journey over to see Tina. He peers in her door to see a professional "thirty-something" woman sitting behind the desk. Her blond hair is groomed nicely, and her simple but striking appearance has Marty staring. "Come on in and sit down, Marty," she says. "I hear your group is having some problems."

Marty isn't sure he likes that statement, but he's in a "mell of a hess" so he will talk to her about it and get her advice. Tina seems to have a good crew and perhaps he can learn something from her.

Tina explains she has hired the best in the field. She has to pay top dollar, but it's worth it—the team members are all top performers. Customers have nothing but good things to say about their work, attitude, effort, and follow through.

"I suggest you invest the time to find the best people possible," she advises. "If you don't, you wind up paying for it in the end when you have to let them go and find replacements."

Marty sits there looking sheepish. He knows he has made a huge mistake. Tina can tell something is bothering him, so she politely asks if he wants to share what's on his mind. "Are you all right, Marty?" she asks.

He finally gets the nerve to talk about it with her and divulges his failed plan. "I didn't hire the best FSEs for a reason," he says. He talks about how he has structured things so there won't be any threats to his new position. That's the way he's most comfortable with building a team.

Tina asks if he's happy with the way things are now.

"Of course not," he replies.

"Well, take a look at my organization," she says. "People rave about my FSEs." In fact, both Tina and her FSEs get compliments on their work. Tina doesn't see that as a threat, but as a tribute to her ability to hire and develop the right people.

In fact, if one of her people were to get promoted, she views it as a direct result of her guidance, development and mentorship. Like a teacher with a successful student, she has helped them develop and now they are off to bigger and better things.

Marty hasn't viewed things like this. This is interesting. "But what do I do now with what I have to work with?" he asks Tina. "Things are really a mess."

Tina thinks a minute and asks Marty if he had set expectations with the group when they arrived. "Did you set standards they should achieve?" she asks. He replies he had. Tina's point is they should be working to these standards regardless of their past. If they don't perform to these levels, then get them help so they can achieve these goals. If they won't or can't do the work, then put them on performance review and get them to shape up or ship out. Marty thanks Tina and leaves to return to his office.

He is glad he spoke with Tina and solicited her opinion. Marty thinks more about what she said and how he should implement "Operation Clean Sweep"—increase the quality or decrease the quantity of his people. He has to prepare for the possibility that he could lose people. Some of his FSEs may not make the standards adjustment. There has to be enforcement of a standard to bring them to a level of performance so the complaints stop.

Marty introduces these standards to his people. Some work to achieve them and others complain and suffer through performance reviews. Marty winds up losing two people because they can't adapt. He hears about two others who are looking to make a job change and may be gone soon.

After thinking back on what has happened and the wisdom he learned from Tina, Marty wishes he had hired the best candidates possible. He may have had some problems with the group, but he couldn't imagine anything as bad as what he is going through now. He realizes he shouldn't worry about protecting his job. As Tina commented, she is proud to see her people do well and the area VP has complimented her and her team.

Marty shouldn't have worried about being the *Best of Breed* in the first place.

Identifying

The *Best of Breed* is truly a unique personality type. In the corporate workplace they may be perceived as *Retired on the Job* or one who doesn't care about their job. Don't make the same mistake. The *Best of Breed* exhibits certain business traits that play a key role in identifying this worker. They are as follows:

- Forms a team of workers who perform below company standards
- Is usually in management
- Was successful as an individual contributor
- Employs unorthodox hiring practices
- Hires substandard employees
- Experiences exceptionally high number of complaints regarding his team

Another area for identification is to benchmark the *Best of Breed's* team against a peer group. This will be the final piece of critical data to assist in the identification process. If this team appears far inferior to others, then you have made positive identification.

Interaction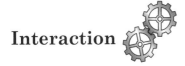

It's difficult to deal with someone who has decided on a substandard approach to business. This can be very disruptive in achieving both personal and company objectives. The best approach is to be polite and respectful. This will help the *Best of Breed* feel comfortable with others in the workplace. If you can create an environment where the *Best of Breeds* let down their guard, then you may be able to coach them into rebuilding their team for excellence.

If you are like Sam, then you will probably realize it's pointless to fight with a personality like this. Aggressively dealing with them will only lead to frustration and continued poor performance. If your approach becomes too aggressive, use caution since the *Best of Breed* will most likely respond with conflict and aggression of their own.

Partners/Political Alliances

The *Best of Breed* won't have many corporate partners. Because they work and hire out of fear, they have a tendency to be loners and rarely welcome others into their incompetent world.

If any personalities create an alliance with them, it will likely be a *Gluteus Maximizer*. The *Best of Breed* can appreciate the accolades from this smooching personality.

The *Best of Breed* will try to impress any authority figure that will give them praise or brownie points. The goal is to position themselves for stability and long-term promotions.

Long-term Effects

Unless an organization wants managers to hire substandard people to make themselves look good, the outcomes can be harsh for the *Best of Breed*. In a normal situation, they don't succeed in their careers unless they quickly see their misguiding management style and take actions to correct it.

Over time and without correction, this personality will be looking for employment elsewhere.

In today's demanding corporate environment, they will be able to hide from upper management for only so long. Mediocre results and inadequate work methods will quickly catch the eye of company executives looking to improve the bottom line. Once discovered, these personalities will find themselves being micro managed towards improvement.

Because the *Best of Breed* was successful as an individual, there is hope for turnaround as a leader. Having close guidance and being constantly measured for refinement will be keys for development.

Not that I'm complaining, but I'll tell you what I find particularly difficult to believe: we're actually guarding garbage.

Armed and Dangerous

The Corporate Ladder
(Climbing Up Others' Backs to Success)

The Personality

There are many determined individuals in the corporate world. Some get ahead through hard work and the results from it. Others are prepared to get a leg up wherever and whenever they can. They view all others as subjects ready to lend a hand to get over the castle wall—ready for the next promotion. They look at their co-workers and see rungs on their backs, constructed for climbing so the *Corporate Ladder* can get a little higher up in the corporate food chain.

The Story

William is whistling the song from Huey Lewis and the News, "Jacob's Ladder": "Step by step, rung by rung..." He's on a mission to climb the Corporate ladder at Digitron and he whistles this particular song to keep him focused on his next promotion. It's the motivation he needs to keep heading in an upward direction.

He views everyone at work as having rungs on their back. In fact, to keep his climbing sharp for a day at the office he practices scaling telephone poles in his front yard. William is always careful to stay clear of the transformer. He remembers what happened to his uncle when full attention wasn't given to this task during climbing sessions. While atop the pole, his uncle became distracted by a passing bird and laid his hands right on top of the transformer. The shock was so intense his uncle's fillings were smoldering for two days after the incident.

William's climbing practices aren't for exercise. He wants to be able to get that leg up in a hurry if an opportunity to get ahead at work presents itself. Many times he has to remember to take off his climbing shoes before coming to the office for fear of inflicting severe damage to one of his co-workers.

William is a sharp sales manager for the plastics division of Digitron located in Sacramento, California. A short, lean and scrappy man in his early thirties, he has three years of sales management and four years of corporate sales under his belt. He believes he's primed and ready for the next step, Director of Sales Operations for the Western Region. He has this title within his sights and can't help but think of the possibilities: money, recognition, and most of all stature. Getting the director position is like drinking from the Holy Grail. His goals in life will be achieved if he can just get the promotion.

He remembers how he obtained his first sales position and whom he had to beat out. Janice Tillman, he recalls vividly, is the one he was victorious over.

Janice was angry and very disappointed when she didn't get the position. She was set on starting a sales career at Digitron. He got to know her a little before the interview while they both sat in the lobby filling out the fifty-page application and waiting to be called for the interview.

Janice had a little climbing history of her own. She wore sharp stiletto heels that can dig in when needed, and she pictured everyone with handrails on their back.

"No sense in waiting to get promoted." she said. "You have to seize life by the..."

She was cut off in mid-sentence as her name was called for her to be interviewed. Janice left to do battle behind closed doors, while William remained to contemplate her words.

He had to have a strategy to get the job. There was only one open sales position and he was determined to get it. Fresh out of college and still wet behind the ears, he was going to beat out Janice—who had a year of experience—and any other candidates for the job.

William remembered his first interview at Digitron like it was only a few months ago. He was wearing his sharp pin-stripe blue suit and was prepared for any question. After thoroughly studying Digitron's products and services, examining their mission statement, and investigating the competition, William was ready for the killer interview. He hit it off with the Director of Sales, Spud Wilson.

Spud was a short guy, but full of energy and spunk. After a few minutes, William discovered Spud had worked hard to achieve his position, but didn't have a degree.

"William, an incredible opportunity like this happens only once in a person's lifetime," Spud stated.

"The fluff is really flowing now," William thought. "I will just listen attentively, ask some questions, and get along with him."

The interview went well and after a few thank you letters and phone calls, William got the job. He could only imagine how upset Janice must have been when she was told she didn't win. *Çe la vie.*

"Digitron must think I can really blaze trails for them, so that's why they made me the offer," William proudly recited to himself. This was his first position in the corporate world.

After quickly learning the ropes, his first four years in direct sales were outstanding. He set new records and put in the extra effort to ensure success. Upper management took notice of William.

Phil, the current manager, is retiring and William believes he's the number one replacement choice. He recalls some of the stories Phil shared with him. The sharing was prompted after an event William witnessed.

On a nice spring day a few years ago, he saw Phil jogging without a shirt on during the lunchtime break. What William really noticed were the marks on Phil's back. William knew Phil didn't serve in the military, but recalled Phil's wife Suzie loved cats. Was Phil a human scratching post for those cats? He pictured Phil at home running for the phone with five or six cats on his back, claws dug in, holding on for their lives. William recalled *Meet the Parents,* a movie he saw, and wondered if Phil did any cat milking.

The next day over lunch, William asked Phil about the marks on his back.

"That's a good observation. Let me share a story with you," Phil replied.

He shared with William that management isn't all glory. Sometimes he feels his back is about to break with all the *Gluteus Maximizers* and *Corporate Ladder* climbers hanging all over him.

"It's their toe holds, spiked shoes, and climbing equipment that made those marks," Phil disgustedly said. "I get so frustrated with these people. I have to constantly yell, 'Get off!'" he exclaimed. "Then I head to the chiropractor. If at all possible, avoid these personality types."

William thanked Phil for sharing his experience with these people.

"I've seen a lot during my time as an employee in the department," he thought. "I will make an excellent manager with all of this knowledge."

William learns careful consideration is being given to hire the right candidate for the soon-to-be-open sales manager position. Digitron is under scrutiny from the local community for promoting enough women into management.

William catches wind of this from the office gossiper and won't accept these conditions. Climbing the corporate ladder is very important, and he has worked too hard the past four years to be successful.

Gertrude, an internal candidate with two years of sales experience, is working in a different sales channel. Based on her background and the Corporate focus, she appears to be the most qualified candidate.

The difference between the two candidates is their sales success. While William sets sales records, Gertrude consistently performs slightly over quota each month.

Additionally, the cardinal rule at Digitron is don't promote the top sales person. They typically are greedy and too self-centered to put themselves aside for the team. This philosophy is based on the needs of the one outweighing the needs of the many.

It looks as if Gertrude will get the job. "Not by the hair of my chinny chin chin," William thinks while gently scratching his chin. The real wolf is coming out in him.

Over his career, William has networked with his peers as well as upper management. There's a favor owed to him by upper management and it's time to play this card. He had helped cover up commission fraud the previous year. Issues like this are dealt with severe penalties and if discovered, someone will surely lose their job. William came to the rescue. He worked to ensure details of this were kept quiet and the issue seemed to vanish into thin air.

Because of his cooperation to support the cover-up of unethical behavior combined with his relationship with upper management, William is awarded the sales manager position. Condoning unethical behavior has allowed him to succeed over another candidate. He feels a person can get away with this once and avoid getting caught. However, climbing the corporate ladder is just too important; he would repeat his cover-up if the opportunity arose again.

After six months in the new job, William is feeling good. He has just finished his sales manager month-end reports and tells his staff, "If you all can turn another great performance like last month, that would be great." (Some of William's staff imagine a scene from the movie *Office Space:* "What's happening Peter? I need you to come in tomorrow and again on Sunday to help catch up." If William walked around with a cup of coffee and suspenders on, it would be a perfect match.)

He has been struggling with a new way to motivate his team. He is torn between the Alec Baldwin approach from *Glengarry Glen Ross* and the Lumbergh approach from *Office Space.* Because William's personality isn't built for screaming and "in your face" cursing, he decides the Lumberg approach is best—soft-spoken, but to the point. Things are good in his department with his newfound sales motivation techniques, but William wants more. A few years have passed and he needs another promotion. William thrives on climbing the corporate ladder and thirsts for another boost to his ego.

"With my background and proven results, I am the best fit for the open director's position," he believes. A legend in his own mind. What better choice is there?

However, time and his pursuit for climbing the corporate ladder catch up to him. During final interviews, the vice president of sales—who has been recently informed of the commission fraud overlooked by William a year ago—asks a very direct question.

"William, can you tell me why you would be a good fit for the director position considering you concealed a known Company violation involving commission fraud?" the VP asks.

William is dumbfounded and knows his ladder is about to collapse. Speechless, he can only hand over his Company badge and wait for Corporate security to pursue the information it needs to put him away. It looks like William may need a new ladder.

Identifying

The steps the *Corporate Ladder* takes to get ahead may leave you a bit confused in trying to identify this personality. Here are their characteristics:

- Is extremely driven to succeed
- Is known to exhibit unethical behavior
- Expresses little regard for those who can't assist in getting ahead
- Adapts well to win over competitors and works overtime to succeed in new position—a good corporate climber
- Craves promotion

A common misstep that can throw you off the trail of recognizing this personality type is their work ethic. On the surface the *Corporate Ladder* may look like the *Workaholic*. However, the key difference between the two is their focus on getting ahead. *Workaholics* excel through their work and results, but their passion is their work. The *Corporate Ladder's* sole mission is to get ahead at any cost.

Another personality they resemble is the *Gluteus Maximizer*. While *Gluteus* takes the soft approach to smooching, the *Corporate Ladder* takes a more rigid climbing stance and digs in with both feet.

Interaction

Understanding the drive and desires of the *Corporate Ladder* is only the first step. Aligning oneself with this personality can be a good political move towards your career. If you witness unethical behavior, immediately disassociate yourself from the *Corporate Ladder* and inform management. Becoming too emotionally attached to getting promoted may find you facing unemployment.

To avoid conflict with the *Corporate Ladder*, stay out of the way of an aggressive "ladder climber" and maintain continuous and honest conversation. Being up front about your own objectives and lines of integrity will help establish a healthy relationship with clear boundaries.

"Ladder climbers" need backs to prop them up. They require a solid foundation of co-workers so they can ascend another rung on the corporate ladder.

Partners/Political Alliances

Corporate Ladders align themselves with as many strategic co-workers as possible. The *Ladder's* efforts are spent networking and building trust with peers and upper management to create strong strategic relationships with the executive team.

The *Napoleon* is an alliance they seek. Putting in hard work will be appreciated by a *Napoleon* and this may enable them to skip a few rungs on the corporate ladder.

Long-term Effects

Like William, if *Corporate Ladders* continue on an unethical path, they will find the security department knocking on their office doors to offer unemployment. Although not every *Corporate Ladder* personality will end up with the same fate, the long-term effects from associating with this personality can feel like being imprisoned. Associates can feel trapped in a situation of being overworked, misguided, and stepped on while the *Corporate Ladder* pursues the mission of reaching a goal at any cost.

This personality has the right direction and motivation, but must sustain integrity and honesty to become a long-term employee and valuable contributor to a company's overall success.

The Untouchables
(Protected by an Authority Figure)

The Personality

In some companies there's a group of individuals who management creates and supports as the gatekeepers to specific information. This unique group retains the right to collect questions from the field and seek answers within the corporation. Workers quickly find there's little substance to the information they hold and accountability runs thin.

It's apparent why this group is allowed to exist within a corporation. Their fragile fiefdom is created so an empire builder will have a kingdom to rule.

Challenging such a group is futile as they retain a certificate of protection from their ruler. Questioning them is like shooting arrows at their sovereign. Thus is born *The Untouchables.*

The Story

Ben transfers to the corporate offices of Digitron. He is happy to still be working with such a large and prestigious Company. After all, their digits are the most widely sought out in the industry. He was stationed at the Nome, Alaska branch for three years and has seen how diligent the workers are at Digitron— especially Ron who got all those digits dug out of the frozen tundra.

In his mid-twenties, Ben doesn't have the joint problems more senior employees have in the Nome climate. His agile body glides through the mountains of snow and ice to arrive safely at his desk. His short-cropped hair and lean body don't provide much insulation from the weather. However, his long stride cuts the walk from the parking lot into seconds.

Ben's first assignment is to work with Rudy who has been at Corporate for a few months. The two meet and get along very well. They have similar backgrounds and ethical work habits. Rudy shows Ben around and informs him who the players are at headquarters.

He is curious what Rudy means by "players."

"Don't you know, Ben?" Rudy replies. "These are the players of the corporate game, and you are at home court now. The corporate players are those who play games to get by in their jobs, have fun, and get ahead. Where have you been? There are a lot of different players. *Gluteus Maximizers, Napoleons, Ascendo Inabilituses;* the list goes on and on. Be aware and keep your eyes open. In fact, there are some major players over there. *The Untouchables.*"

"What, or who, is that?" asks Ben.

Rudy explains, "They are a group who is protected by an authority figure. Their work performance is substandard, but they are allowed to function and flourish due to their corporate sponsor."

"What?" Ben exclaims. "I'm not sure what you mean."

"Let me explain more about this," Rudy replies. "A good example is the Clarence Beaks character on the movie *Trading Places.* Untouchable, so he thinks—Clarence goes about his business his way without regard to anyone else. In the end, his untouchable organization falls hard."

Rudy explains his experience with Dan, the *Cover Up* and Dan's organization, *The Untouchables.* Rudy has spent considerable time with his boss, Beth, understanding this organization. She shared with him, and now he will share with Ben, what these people are all about.

He explains an authority figure governs an empire. Depending on how they rule determines whether they are a corporate player. One such ruler is the *Napoleon.* They rule their empire with an iron fist and want things done their way. Corporate may have their ideas on how the organization is to be run, but the *Napoleon* modifies it and operates to benefit their kingdom.

The Untouchables go about business their own way and are supported by an authority figure. Ben finds out more as he starts to work with them and obtains additional coaching from Rudy on how to handle this interaction.

He advises Rudy how to steer clear of this organization.

"This organization was created to collect inept people who

support an authority figure so they will have an empire of followers," Rudy explains. "This is a self-perpetuating kingdom. If you need accurate, timely information, seek the true information source and avoid *The Untouchables* whenever possible."

Ben has to work with *The Untouchables* in some circumstances. It's an eerie feeling being in those halls of slackness. He feels he has to take a shower after listening to their babble being substituted for real knowledge. Ben is strong and learns to work through these issues.

He has learned he can't fight city hall. He shouldn't lodge complaints with the head of *The Untouchables* because that organization is protected from high within the corporation. The top supports the feeble bottom, which are *The Untouchables*.

In fact, *The Untouchables* are creating work for themselves. They jump on project bandwagons to act as corporate liaisons. Ben experiences this work creation (or actual existence justification) firsthand.

Ben works with *The Untouchables* on one memorable project. There is a corporate change about to occur which will make several important modifications to some field staff: the digit support staff throughout the country is being reorganized. *The Untouchables* are involved in this implementation. The Corporation has an opinion this field group's job responsibility lies in one area while it actually is totally different. Where in the world did they get this idea? They got it from (whom else?) *The Untouchables*. They overemphasize the situation so their own support appears critical. This creates a more secure position for them. Ben feels lucky to have witnessed this spin tactic. He wouldn't have learned this unique approach without the opportunity to work closely with *The Untouchables*.

He also sees people jockeying for power within this organization. Some belittle others to diminish their roles while a few form alliances with co-members to increase their power and worth. It's like a den of thieves—who can be trusted?

Ben, Rudy and other co-workers are forced to work with *The Untouchables* in some situations, but they minimize their interactions when possible. They think through their requests and interactions to avoid strife with this group. Rudy points out to Ben that *The Untouchable* organization is full of *Cover Ups*. Anyone who challenges their jobs or performance has the tables turned on them to look like they don't perform their own job properly. It's an 180-degree assault.

Thinking about this tactic, Ben sees why they do this. Their effort and results don't warrant much merit; so they rely on spin, cover-up, and outright lies.

Ben learns the ropes quickly. He appreciates his co-worker Rudy for pointing out this group, and more importantly, how to work without causing strife with them. With their power emanating high within the organization, creating a standoff could result in corporate suicide.

Identifying

Like the *Cover Up*, not every organization has the privilege of having such an esteemed group of individuals—as *The Untouchables*—in their organization. Tracking and identification isn't difficult once the proper protective markings are discovered. These are similar to the *Cover Up* and include:

- Perform work they choose to do on their own schedule
- Include many *Cover Ups* in the group
- Allow work to pile up as they modify requested priorities
- Possess minimal training or skills for the work they support
- Enjoy close ties to an authority figure—for protection in return for acting as additional subjects in the kingdom
- Respond with venomous action to anyone challenging their work or output

Interaction

As discussed above, many *Untouchable* groups serve as gatekeepers to larger groups holding valuable information. They are the liaisons working with internal knowledge groups. With their lack of skills and worth to their customers, *The Untouchables* challenge anyone questioning their ethics or output. They possess a "get out of jail free card" from their corporate sponsor—their authority figure.

With these facts, employees know to work around this organization to avoid confrontation. The results of a frontal assault are ugly as *The Untouchables'* authority figure steps in to protect the flock. Seeking direct knowledge resources— as Ben learned to do—is the best solution for companies having an *Untouchable* organization. These groups know they are untouchable and make no qualms about letting people know it.

An important point to remember is to ensure the knowledge group you directly approach doesn't have close ties to this organization. Inquire to obtain history on your resource to see if they have an association with *The Untouchables* and if some one has been burned in the past. Don't be the guinea pig.

Partners/Political Alliances

The Untouchables will partner with authority figures such as *Napoleons*. They exist to serve a purpose for someone higher in the corporate food chain.

Other groups such as *Gluteus Maximizers* may want to form alliances with *The Untouchables* in order to find a way into the authority figure's grace. *The Untouchables* are work-ing an avenue they know provides shelter and warrants favors from authority figures.

Long-term Effects

If there's a change in leadership, *The Untouchables* lose their sponsorship. This creates vulnerability and expendability. Based on the number of complaints, *The Untouchables* may take a hard fall. They will have lost their protector who shields them against the arrows of employees challenging them to do their job properly. If they survive, they must scramble to create new ties of assurance.

It's best to keep in good favor of *The Untouchables*, but don't become a close tie. Should the group encounter hardship, those closely affiliated could experience a similar fate.

Mr. Madison, what you just said is one of the most insanely, idiotic things that I have ever heard. At no point in your rambling, incoherent response were you even close to anything that can be considered a rational thought. I award you no points and may God have mercy on your soul.

Billy Madison

The Know-it-all
(Knows All and Shares All)

The Personality

Many families and corporations have members who have experienced many things, been most everywhere, and of course know everything. Most of them don't just retain this information and share when requested; they force this fountain of knowledge onto anyone who dares step into their information library.

There are two distinct breeds of the *Know-it-all* personality. One takes a proactive approach to ensure others are fully aware of their scholarly ways. The other breed is more subtle, acknowledging they know something in order to avoid a conversation. This second breed uses their depth of understanding to ward off intruders that may steal precious minutes of their day engaging them in useless conversation.

This personality avoids topics they know little about and replies with vague, general statements so they won't diminish their self-appointed head librarian status. Leveraging their knowledge is key to their personal success, so they seek conversations to apply their worldly experience.

This can be one of the most annoying personalities known. Listening to a *Know-it-all* can be agonizing torture.

The Story

Diane and Bill—both sales representatives—are in the midst of a Company restructuring. Diane now has to work with Bill in a new territory. Although the challenge of this change is very exciting and opportunistic, it certainly comes with consequences.

"This is the most dysfunctional reorganization I have ever seen," Diane thinks. "I have witnessed more organized stampedes. The field now has to live with this mess."

Prior to this mayhem, each sales rep was responsible for their success and compensated accordingly. After spending eight years at Digitron, Diane has lost all enthusiasm for change. She knows most Company policies and is well-connected throughout the organization.

Diane is a junior sales rep and Bill is the senior she will now work with. With the Company change, Diane's sales will now automatically roll up and positively impact Bill's pocket book. She is basically working for Bill.

"How are you feeling about the changes, Diane?" Bill asks.

"I'm doing fine," she sarcastically replies. "I knew this was going to happen several months ago."

"How did you know that?" he asks.

"There isn't much I don't know," Diane conceitedly comments.

Bill has a great attitude towards work. He always contributes 110% to the job. Bill's only quirk is he expects everyone else in the office to give the same effort, and he has a hard time accepting those who don't.

"Why can't everyone just work like they are supposed to?" he thinks.

Bill is very frustrated with some salespeople's lack of commitment. Because of his compulsive, self-indulged behavior, most of the department thinks Bill should be committed to some asylum. He and Bryan, the *F.A.D.* (before he was fired) used to hang around the office all night long working on projects they didn't finish during the day. *F.A.D.* was killing trees while Bill was working on sales strategies.

Diane is enthusiastic and committed, but with this new change she isn't very open to the new ideas Bill suggests. Even though she is a team player of sorts, her knowledge of the Company and accounts has developed her into someone with little patience. She is tired of the detailed monotony of working with some salespeople. It's a simple process. Why can't they see it?

Bill prepares to call on his accounts. With this new structure, he feels it will be wise to have Diane accompany him. The customers should get to know them as a team and she could assist him with the sale. After all, two heads are better than one.

"Diane," Bill says. "I'm going on a new appointment and I'd like you to be there to learn about this customer."

"Who is it?" she asks.

"Our largest potential customer yet, Cuplanetics, Inc.," Bill replies.

"Oh, I already know about them. Besides, I have other things to do," Diane snidely comments.

Bill is a bit surprised by Diane's response, but this isn't the first time she has passed on learning more about an opportunity. She seems to always know something about everything. Even during Company events or in a social environment, Diane knows it all. It's rare that anyone in the office can share a personal or professional experience without Diane adding her two cents worth: "Yeah, yeah," "I know," "I've done that too," or worse, "Let me tell you more about that."

Diane has done it all. She has been everywhere and done everything; or so she says. Most of her co-workers feel taxed from her knowledge-sharing tactics. She loves to walk around, share all her knowledge, and the employees scatter like she has the plague. Even old Rufus—who can hardly move— makes a beeline for the men's room when Diane heads his way. He has safe haven in there from her (at least so far).

After Bill returns from his appointment, he runs into Diane and shares with her the details of his customer meeting.

"Diane," Bill says, "I would like to discuss with you how our meeting went, my strategy for positioning the right product to sell them, and the roll-out schedule."

"I'm sure I have a good idea of what they want, so just shoot me a quick summary email and I will take care of it," she snaps.

This is really starting to upset Bill, because Diane doesn't have a clue what Bill or the customer needs. He feels his blood pressure rising in proportion with the frustration level of working with such a callous individual.

"Diane, I really need your full attention so we can take care of this new customer," he retorts. "Here is what I need..." Bill says as he is cut off in mid sentence.

"I know, I know," she replies. "They want the product and you want me to do the administrative work and the roll-out schedule, right? And by the way, I am going to be working on a special project so I may not have time," she replies, walking off.

Again, Bill is flabbergasted and isn't sure what his next steps are going to be. Not only does Diane disregard both the customer's and his needs, but also changes the subject and walks off without any respect for Bill or regard for the situation.

Bill consults with his manager about the situation. From Bill's detailed description of Diane's actions, the manager conveys he is dealing with a *Know-it-all*.

"If Diane can't be in control of a conversation, she finds a way to leave," the manager states.

Now in this new role, Bill supervises her work without having any authority. This places him in an interesting predicament. He requests his manager speak with Diane and set her straight on her new role and responsibilities. This awkward reorganization has sales dealing with many new challenges.

Identifying

It may take several encounters with a *Know-it-all* to assimilate inherent nuances and properly identify the personality. They have the uncanny ability to relate to many different discussions and can connect with multiple personality types. Their traits include:

- Typically "knowing more" than anyone in the office about a multitude of topics
- Being very relational—adaptable to all interoffice discussions involving topics on which they have expertise
- Readily joining discussions then dominating with their own experience
- Overwhelming others with facts
- Wanting to outclass anyone's knowledge or experience in any discussion
- Frequently responding with "Yeah, yeah" or "I've done that before"
- Avoiding conversational topics they know little about

This personality has the unique ability to divert conversations back onto themselves to seize control and regain the limelight.

Interaction

There is a challenge working with this personality as they consider themselves very knowledgeable. They can be unwilling to consider other's opinions and contributions. Seizing control is one of their traits. Co-workers or staff may encounter a scramble for power when working with the *Know-it-all*. If this occurs when working on a team business project, it's best to avoid conflict and let management settle disputes. Personal discussion differences can be dealt with by walking away or avoiding the discussion with this person altogether.

Know-it-alls are very likeable at first impression and usually connect with most people around them. They have a lot in common with everyone. But after getting to know them, you will discover they have had more unique experiences than anyone and are an expert on multiple subjects.

A great strategy in working successfully with this personality is to recognize them early, realize it's nothing personal, and take everything they say for what it's worth. Another good move is not to challenge them or try to outdo them with personal experiences. The *Know-it-all* covets being the centerpiece of discussions, presentations, and meetings and may even, without invitation, join co-workers around the coffee station for an early morning chat.

Partners/Political Alliances

Know-it-alls don't have many political alliances and it's advised to use caution aligning too closely with them. They may rub co-workers the wrong way, especially upper management who prefer employees who are interested in learning and developing.

Alignment with a *Napoleon* is a challenge for this personality. The *Napoleon* wants actual work performed, not fluff and talk of having done it. They are building a kingdom and don't need any bragging serfs.

Long-term Effects

Over time *Know-it-alls* will have difficultly advancing their careers and building strong internal and external relationships. In the end they may even find themselves without any friends or support—just as Diane may if she doesn't become more flexible and open to new ideas.

Although *Know-it-alls* can bring excitement, fun and a unique personality to the corporate office, the caution here is their long-term effects can lead to disruption to the interoffice and company goals.

That's an interesting color.
Did you pick it?

No, the guy at the counter did. Why?

Well, they say that geniuses pick the color
green.

Oh.

But, you didn't pick it.

Meet the Parents

The Micro Manager
(Watching Every Step)

The Personality

Just as an entomologist studies insects through a magnifying glass, the *Micro Manager* studies employees. Everything is observed and timed. They expect the highest performance from all. No rock goes unturned as they walk the aisles observing everything.

The amount of extra work is enormous, as they demand report after report to examine every detail from six different angles. Morale runs low. Very few see the point of this supreme effort only to justify to the *Micro Manager* the job is being performed properly. Their method of supervision is usually management through intimidation.

The Story

"This is the third time I've asked you for this report, Dave," George barks. "What's it going to take for you to complete your work on time? One more late delivery and I'm putting you on written warning!"

George is 5'9" and his snappy attitude is so intimidating people avoid him at any cost. His beady eyes, fit frame, and high intensity personality makes working with him arduous. George's loud bark has everyone cowering in their cubes.

As Dave walks away from the growling manager, he's convinced this guy is out of hand with his extreme observation and measurement of everything and everyone. "I'm surprised there aren't shoplifting mirrors around the department!" Dave thinks. Dave wouldn't be surprised if there's a camera watching him right now with George on the other end, policing activity.

George thinks of his people as serfs who are there to serve the kingdom. It's his job to ensure they perform and need to be closely monitored with their results scrutinized. He feels his employees are incompetents. If only he were allowed to bring in a whip to work; then they would feel how intent he is for them to do their work.

Dave normally doesn't have a difficulty turning in his reports on time, but the count is now up to five per day. With the high quotas and sales challenges, he needs all the extra time he can get to overachieve. Dave is required to complete the high quantity of reports each day thanks to his year-to-date performance and George's close supervision. By 10:00 a.m. each day he submits reports detailing teleprospecting, appointments, daily to-do list, sales tracker, and customer follow up.

"Who can read all this crap?" Dave thinks. "George needs a staff of ten just to sift through all that paper and make some sense of the reports. It seems like an exercise just to make sure the employees are doing something related to work."

The time and effort put into the reports leave him about four hours each day to sell. In addition, Dave is required to spend a half hour every day reporting to George via conference call on the day's activities. Can you say "micro management?"

George is known throughout the office as being the strong authority type. He is called the "slave driver" in offsite beverage discussions. Never afraid to speak his mind with the team, George is constantly demanding more production while keeping the team at bay. One day these guys will turn on him. He's like a prison warden maximizing the punishment on the inmates, which in this case are sales people.

The following day, George walks over to Steve who's hard at work writing up another report.

"Steve, how many calls did you make today?" George inquires.

"I made fifteen," Steve replies.

"Fifteen? Are you kidding? I just finished listening to fifteen messages in the past hour. How is it possible you made only fifteen calls during an eight hour period?" George barks.

"Sorry sir, but with the amount of reports you require from us each day my time is limited for prospecting," Steve responds.

"Reports," George retorts. "Thanks for reminding me. I believe yours was late today. Consider yourself on written warning and don't let it happen again."

The staff imagines themselves chained to their desks with the phones glued to their hands. If they don't make a phone call quickly the fast busy tone will chime—alerting George that a lazy, no-good sales serf isn't doing their job. He storms out of his office, bull whip in hand thinking a good crack will remind those serfs who is boss and what they should be doing.

It's easy to dream of this scenario and it's not just Dave doing all the imagining. The entire team trades these type stories. Just the other day Mike—another member of the sales team—commented he could see mountains of paperwork as each salesperson churned out reports. Conveyers transport the paper to George's office with each one time-stamped just before arriving. Anything overdue by even one second results in the harshest punishment. Mike can see sales serfs hung by their thumbs for neglecting details like this.

George is a true motivator at heart, but has a hard time delivering the message without the fear built into it. An ex-Marine, George constantly beats his people for more production. The team's production continues to fall while the paperwork piles higher and higher in George's in-box.

He knows these guys wouldn't stand up to five minutes in the field unless he sets them straight. He believes he's doing this for their own good. It's not his fault turnover is 300% a year. They are just wimps posing as sales people.

George remembers some of the interviews he has conducted. There was one where this timid guy actually ran out of the interview crying like a baby. Was he too scary? "These wimps can't take it and they need to get a life and get to work," he thinks.

George walks over to another member of his team.

"Sam, you incompetent boob," George barks. "I see on your report you forgot to put the time of the call you made. If I see it again consider yourself on verbal warning. By the way, I need another report from you by the close of business tomorrow."

"What type of report?" Sam sheepishly asks.

"I have to present to my boss why we aren't performing and I need ammunition to justify the lack of production," George retorts. "It's beside the fact you guys can't sell! This report needs to show all activity for the past thirty days by account, including sales made. The Company needs sales. If you can't do it and follow my rules, then I will find people who can."

A few minutes later Greg, a seasoned sales executive, walks into the office with a smile on his face.

"What's with that grin?" George snidely inquires. "Did someone sell something?"

"If I was doing any better, you would have to pinch me," Greg replies.

"Good news?" George scoffs. "Happen to make quota yet?"

Greg runs his hands through his hair and prepares to deliver the good news.

"Actually I just closed this huge deal with a local company," Greg cheerfully replies. "I stole the business from our largest competitor by using creative sales tactics."

"That's great. How did you do it?" George inquires.

"I used our current pricing and promised the customer I would hand deliver the products to their front door next week," Greg continues. "That's the type of service this customer is looking for."

An angry scowl develops like a rain cloud over George's face.

"What!" George barks. "Are you kidding me? You know sales reps don't hand deliver anything to the customer—that's Willy's job in product delivery. This is Company policy and you will have to inform the customer we won't commit to this. If it happens again, consider yourself on written warning."

The echo of the derriere chewing can still be heard as George is off to verbally lacerate another victim. Greg turns and leaves the office a beaten man, not knowing where to turn for encouragement.

Identifying

The identification of a *Micro Manager* is simple. The traits of this corporate personality are:

- Intensive reporting requirements
- Close examination of all work
- Strict operation with no questioning of authority
- Severe repercussions for anyone falling outside the established orders
- Fear management style

You will find intense attention to detail and demand for an extreme amount of reporting are clear signs of a *Micro Manager*. In addition, look for outrageous responses when out-of-the-box thinking is used in an attempt to complete a project.

This personality may surface in most managers at one time or another. The most common instance tends to be when employees are underperforming and they need closer supervision to be successful.

Interaction

Finding a successful working relationship with a *Micro Manager* can be very challenging. Their demand for reports, attention to an overabundance of details, and their inability to welcome empowerment of employees is practically impossible to overcome. However, all hope isn't lost.

The first step is to stick to deadlines and become detail-oriented yourself. Restate in writing exactly what the *Micro Manger* is asking for so the information delivered meets expectations. Personal documentation of your production and results achieved could prove critical to avoiding your next written warning. Having the requests in writing is important to remove any vagueness in a questionable situation.

Inviting *Micro Managers* to become more involved with your daily activities may also be a beneficial way to win them over. Once an employee exceeds company requirements there may be a chance for this personality to back off on the reporting regimen and free up additional time for you to handle normal duties.

Obtaining a full understanding of what makes the *Micro Manager* tick is the first step towards avoiding conflict. They like to manage with authority, fear and pressure. It's their belief this type of management will build a disciplined team of driven overachievers. Quite often the opposite happens. The de-motivating style of this personality drives many to give up and resign or transfer.

Your manager may become a *Micro Manager* if you are underperforming in your position. They are forced to scrutinize your actions at a detailed level in the hopes they can improve your performance.

Partners/Political Alliances

Micro Managers attempt to partner with *Napoleons*. Both of them are power-type people. Since *Micro Managers* love power and control, they will look to a higher figure to seek the same common ground. They will encounter the same emotions their team does when being micro managed themselves—loss of empowerment and openness, and a feeling of being deval-ued. The *Napoleon* will keep this personality on a short leash until leash line is earned.

Micro Managers have the hardest time relating to *Retired on the Job*, the *Spin-Doctor,* and especially *F.A.D.* Although the administrative component of *F.A.D.* is a quality they covet, their fluffiness and delegation drive the *Micro Manager* crazy.

Long-term Effects

If the *Micro Manager* continues with their infinitesimal scrutiny, there will be a mutiny or mass team exodus. There is a limit to the tolerance people have with this personality. If they can relax their intense style and gain a better under-standing of their employees, then they have a chance to be-come a successful manager. However, the longer they stay in their micro mode, results will continue to suffer and employee turnover will rise.

If a manager is in a position where they need to micro manage for legitimate reasons, the focus of this management style must be used to improve employee performance. This truly is a delicate balance of power and support.

When *Micro Managers* are able to modify their style to be used only when needed, they should set goals for their team reflecting both the company's objectives and their own. They should empower their people to become creative thinkers and encourage them to share their ideas.

Lastly, *Micro Managers* need to become empathic and channel their emotions in an enthusiastic light. Lifting the fear from their delivery will produce a happy and successful team.

The time has come for someone to put their foot down and that foot is me.

Animal House

The Court Adviser
(Authority Without Responsibility)

The Personality

In every organization there are those who dream of ruling an empire with all of the authority, but none of the responsibility. A unique situation allows this individual to lend helpful hints to the ruling monarchy and witness their advice turn into reality. By whispering in the emperor's ear, the *Court Adviser* personality can exercise and influence their own ideas through the power of rulers without responsibility for failure.

In order to earn such a powerful position within a corporate kingdom, this personality must demonstrate their worth over time and create such a value the head of state seeks no other advice. Suggestions are weighed for value with the monarchy, outcomes are considered, and implemented if the information is worthy. The *Court Adviser* has then become a cloaked ruler without accountability.

The Story

Ken is new to Digitron. He brings with him many years of experience in production line optimization. In his last company, Simplinetics—where the Company motto is "Simple toys for simple minds"—he excelled and Digitron sought out his talents. From an excellent compensation package to a lifetime supply of digits, it was a deal Ken couldn't refuse.

His military reserve training and discipline will help him in his new position as technology consultant. As he meets his new co-workers, they recognize his clean-cut appearance and attitude exemplifies a well-planned approach to work and life. Ken's 5'10" lean but muscular frame and short military-style hair cut along with an air of style, organization and control will earn him respect in his new position.

Reporting directly to Steve, the Vice President of Operations, Ken's enthusiasm almost overwhelms him as the nuances of this Company are discovered. Every day, his active mind churns with creative ideas. He's ready to make a difference.

Ken made a real difference at Simplinetics as a team member who developed the Brain Buster toy—a toy encouraging learning. The toy asks a question and if the player doesn't enter the correct answer, an electrical shock is administered to encourage knowledge. Initially, the toy was a great success and a favorite at parties. Too bad the government banned it.

Ken walks over to the office of his new boss to meet Hank, who has spent two years working for Steve. After introductions, the three discuss the current production situation and of course, bass fishing. "There's nothing like fishing in this area, Ken," Hank comments. "We will have to go out on my boat sometime. I have a cabin on this nice lake in the mountains."

"I'd love to try some bass fishing," Ken replies.

"Before we decide to cut out of work early, let me show you around the plant," Hank continues.

The two take off as Steve returns to the pile of work on his desk. Ken wants to learn about this new department and its employees quickly so he will be knowledgeable and have the ability to manage effectively. As they tour the plant, Ken spends time getting to know Hank. He learns Hank likes to influence Steve's empire through suggestions, many of which have been implemented.

"Over to the left you can see the high-speed digit conveyor system," Hank states. "I'm the one who suggested to Steve how to optimize the system. This has led to an increase in production of 30%. Steve really loves my ideas."

As their walk continues, Hank thinks about his own situation. "Ken may get in the way of what I have worked very hard to create. I have created an actual empire of my own and love the way it runs. When I suggest technical enhancements to Steve, the resulting changes have impact over the whole production facility." Many of these suggestions have been implemented over the past year, but Hank is never responsible for the outcome. He has great authority with little responsibility and doesn't want Ken to change any of this.

Ken learns that last month Hank suggested to Steve they should limit the amount of waste and recycle digits. The department has been letting workers take home faulty digits for their own use. They are used as doorstops, car jacks, even decorative shelf displays. Now with Hank's idea, the digits are melted and remixed in the goo used to create them.

It wasn't a bad suggestion to make this change, but Hank has other motives. He managed a hefty salary increase for himself while he disadvantaged others through this suggested change. Hank loves this control and witnessing the results from his conversations with Steve.

In further discussions with his employees, Ken learns they resent the relationship between Hank and Steve. They know what Hank is up to and see the results of his handiwork. Hank is manipulating a manager through his abilities and suggestions. He's affecting change, and reaping rewards. Hank doesn't hesitate to let his co-workers know when he receives a raise, either.

He has become an expert at manipulating this game and makes sure he goes out of the way to ensure Steve is taken care of technically. Any technical needs or questions Steve has, Hank personally takes care of them. Ken discovers last Tuesday Steve called Hank in his office to fix his computer.

"Steve, why didn't you pick up the phone and call me instead of coming down to my office?" Hank inquires.

"The phone doesn't work and lights are out in my office," he replies. "No power. So why doesn't my computer work?"

Hank has heard of this problem before. A friend of his in customer service refers to this as an "ID 10 T" (also known as an IDIOT) error.

As Ken starts to work with Hank, he realizes he must take care in dealing with the relationship between Hank and Steve. Ken is smart and has witnessed situations like this before. If he rocks the boat, it will be seen as an outsider coming in and trying to take control. He must make the necessary changes delicately and diplomatically so he maintains control of his department. "How can I achieve department goals and see that Hank is not shown any favoritism?" Ken ponders.

He remembers what happened at Simplinetics with another worker who was a *Gluteus Maximizer* and had hooked up closely with the director. The director ran into some trouble of his own and was asked to relocate his office off-premises permanently. Others in the department thought that surgery might be needed to separate the two. That smoocher had a manipulative relationship with his boss, and Ken doesn't want any of his people involved in a similar situation. He wants to make sure none of his employees have an overwhelming relationship with management, use this to their advantage, and have the department and plant co-workers commenting about it. He can't afford to be in the middle of a soap opera.

Ken decides to call Steve and ask for some of his time to learn more about the department.

"Steve, I would like to spend a few minutes understanding the department's goals with you," Ken says. "Is this a good time?"

"Sure Ken, come on down to my office," Steve replies.

Ken makes the journey and meets with Steve to understand three things. First, Ken must understand the Corporate goals for the department; second, Ken must understand Steve's goals for the department; and lastly, Ken must understand Steve's boss's goals for Steve. In addition to this information, Ken also determines Steve's personal support needs and learns more about Hank's support history.

Instead of making comments during this information gathering session, Ken takes the garnered information, reviews it, and sets three objectives to achieve. First, achieve the department's, Steve's, and Steve's boss' goals; second, eliminate any bias and favoritism associated with Steve; and third, establish support guidelines. Obtaining support must be accomplished through set procedures and without impacting Ken's other two objectives. Getting the job done is key. Working on the politics and personalities in the department is secondary.

Ken remembers at Simplinetics when an implemented plan was devastating to one of his good friends. Gomez—a managerial snafu—wrote up a plan to better organize the sanitation-engineering department because he was tired of personally making the rounds every day and motivating his workers to empty every trashcan. Gomez engineered an idea to have each employee stack their loaded trashcans by the door on their way home each day. This would save time and walking, as all the trash would be in close proximity to office doorways, making it easy to collect and dump by his engineers. That idea went over so well that Gomez was promoted to chief of lavatory quality control. Ken doesn't want any promotions like that coming his way, so he has to think this through carefully.

With an outline to achieve the primary objective, Ken focuses on restructuring objectives two and three. It has to be fair to all parties and make sense to those outside the department both in fairness and in concept.

Thinking about the current situation, Ken affirms Hank has created his own corporate kingdom using Steve as the power figure. Ken must show Steve there are other resources available and he must work through Ken to obtain their services. If Steve bypasses Ken, the whole management structure is lost and the chain of command breaks down. For the good of the department, morale, and efficient operation, he must detail these issues and secure Steve's approval.

Next, Ken must put a plan together to better utilize Hank. Hank has been operating in an exclusive support role for some time and needs to focus on other projects to be recognized for his full abilities. He lists Hank's strengths and weaknesses on a sheet of paper and focuses on where these talents would best be utilized. Ken recognizes Hank has problem solving strengths and the ability to ascertain new technologies. Solving "ID 10 T" issues is a waste of his time. Hank will be more valuable to the Company if his support is available across the Corporate enterprise. He will also create and host a new website for technology education so internal customers can seek answers to their questions rather than wait on an already overloaded technology department.

Ken will ensure Hank informs all employees access to the Web site is necessary to obtain information from it. "If your computer doesn't have power, don't call and say the Web site is down." Working in this manner, Hank's strengths will best serve the department and the Company.

Ken calls Steve and asks for an hour of his time to present some of his findings from the past three weeks. Steve agrees and the two meet at 3:00 p.m. in Steve's office.

"Steve, there are three objectives I should be focusing my time on," Ken states. He shares the entire plan with Steve so they can discuss objectives, fine-tune them, and Ken can set out on his mission to enhance the department. Steve also is provided a realization of the varied talent and resources available within the department. He acknowledges there should be contact with Ken before assigning new projects or asking for technological assistance on products or projects. He affirms there is a new management structure in place with

Ken filling those shoes and agrees it's best to work through him in the future.

The plan is finalized and Ken implements the objectives. The two achieve some great things while keeping their employees happy and feeling they are contributing greatly to the department. The department produces at a tremendous level and quality is at an all time high.

Hank seems to be happy in this new role as many employees seek him out for his Web site information. Employees are no longer jealous of an unjust situation and refrain from making statements regarding Hank's past empire-building relationship with Steve.

Identifying

Court Advisers do an excellent job of hiding or disguising their corporate existence. Cloaked by their executive support, this personality is flushed out only through their own mishaps or poor decision-making influence. Key attributes are:

- Affiliates closely with authority figures
- Seeks to rule an empire through an authority figure
- Wants authority without responsibility
- Holds a unique knowledge set to influence authority figure
- Is manipulative, conniving, and sneaky

If you are successful in identifying the *Court Adviser*, you will notice a close affiliation with an authority figure, creating a necessary bond of dependency. They look to create their niche so the authority figure utilizes their talent, and their knowledge provides great results.

In addition, you may see *Court Advisers* influencing the authority figure through comments on their observations. With a strong relationship and trust, many times the authority figure will act on this information, thus giving *Court Advisers* what they want: power without responsibility.

Interaction

It's important for you to note the *Court Adviser* is very politically oriented. Challenging their authority or questioning their motives not only can bring on their wrath but also that of their sponsoring authority figure. Much work turmoil will come to you should you chose to take a stand against this personality. Crossing them or questioning their corporate position either publicly or privately can result in career suicide. Harm can come to those who don't tread lightly. After all, *Court Advisers* tread lightly, but they do carry a big stick—their authority figure.

When working with this personality, it's best to choose a diplomatic role. You will have more success if you don't challenge their authority. Just listen to their ideas and suggestions.

If you feel changes are necessary, then draft up a positive impact document and share with management who the *Court Adviser* doesn't have alliances with. When doing this, be sure there is a positive outcome for all including this personality.

The *Court Adviser's* strengths are strong understandings of the corporate culture and infrastructure. If you have a good working relationship, they can only help in your career path, or to obtain access to critical company information.

Partners/Political Alliances

Court Advisers gravitate towards authority figures including *Napoleons*. They love to make themselves a valuable resource behind the scenes.

They will stay away from other *Court Advisers* since conflicts can arise easily. Both of these people are vying for power within an organization. They will only align themselves with another *Court Adviser* if the pact will help their situation—such as using a strategy or success tactic from a peer in another area who doesn't threaten their own empire.

This personality will avoid the *Corporate Ladder*, *Gluteus Maximizer* and *Ascendo Inabilitus*. There is little to gain from these personalities. *Court Advisers* are trying to gain a leg up for themselves and don't posses the power for this personality to want to align with them.

Long-term Effects

Court Advisers will align themselves with one main authority figure. As mentioned, this is usually a *Napoleon*. If the *Napoleon's* empire crumbles, so does that of the *Court Adviser*.

This personality will then have to rebuild trust and a dependence to be used as a resource with a new authority figure. Depending on the talents of the new authority figure, they may find themselves without an empire or any way to create a new one. It's at that point the *Court Adviser* changes positions, or even companies, looking for a new empire to create.

I only said we'd make it across.
I never said anything about the wheels
staying on.

Road Trip

The Gossiper
(The Rumor Spreader)

The Personality

There always seems to be someone in every office who's intent on spreading news of others in addition to information about the corporation. They thrive on being the messenger of this news and discussing potential outcomes. On close inspection, they are always away from their workstation as their "Pony Express" service keeps them on the run. Work is piled high in their in-box, as they are hard at work broadcasting their news. The *Gossiper* is the emissary of many companies.

The Story

Sam, Julie and Phyllis are standing around the coffee station on a Monday morning. The three are sharing their weekend experiences and talking about what adventures the upcoming workweek may bring.

"I'm so tired," Sam comments. I just hate Mondays."

"Sounds like somebody has a case of the Mondays," Maude mocks as she walks by quoting a line from the movie *Office Space.*

She is around the corner before anyone can say a word. Sam has a disgusted look on his face as Phyllis adds fuel to the fire.

"If someone made a comment like that in my husband's office, they would get their butt kicked."

Sam's look of disgust turns to anger.

"I get so overwhelmed with what I have to do each week," he says in exasperation. "On Monday, the nightmare starts all over again."

"I love Mondays," Julie cheerfully comments. "What a great way to start the week off; a cup of coffee, good times with good friends and I'm still employed."

"The fluff is getting thick," Sam thinks. "It's getting hard to breathe."

"Didn't you hear about Tom down in marketing?" Phyllis enthusiastically interjects. "I hear he's having an affair with a gal in finance. He's been married for more than six years."

Julie thinks about this woman who is involved with a married man.

"I suppose it's not the men in your life that count, it's the life in your men," Julie comments.

"Let me tell you about Don down in shipping," Phyllis continues.

As Phyllis rambles on, Sam feels very awkward having this conversation with her in the break room. He's not interested in this gossip and is concerned about his affiliation with her. Just being around Phyllis and the gossip flowing from her mouth may have others thinking he's contributing to the office rumor mill.

Phyllis has an extremely difficult time keeping anything to herself. Her passion for gossip is like that of a disease of sorts. It's an addiction she can't kick. She gets her high from it. Whether it's personal or business-related, anyone in the office can turn to Phyllis for the latest trash about someone and the latest "inside scoop" on Company information. She invests most of her day spreading the latest rumors to her co-workers. Her agenda is to gain as much knowledge as possible about everyone so she isn't left speechless. When she isn't spreading rumors, she's eavesdropping to collect more gossip for future topics of discussion.

Obviously, Phyllis doesn't get much of her assigned work done since she's out on her missions all day. The work piles up on her abandoned desk as the weeks go by. Her cube is starting to look like a *F.A.D.* storage area.

Later that day, Tom hears about the gossip being spread by Phyllis. Not only is this embarrassing to him, but his colleague in finance is being targeted as well. She just received a promotion and will now be overseeing the auditing group.

"What could be going through the decision maker's mind about this nasty rumor?" Tom thinks. "Could they be doubting their decision to make her a manager? What am I going to do about this mess?"

Caught up in this malicious rumor and untruth, Tom begins to feel trapped and victimized. Will his boss fire him because she thinks he started the rumor? Will his integrity be destroyed in this Company? Who can he turn to? He has no idea who started the rumor and without these details his case appears hopeless. Tom knows his career is being ruined. Rumors spread like wildfire.

Sam decides to approach Tom and share the gossip he has heard from Phyllis.

"Tom, I've heard some nasty rumors from Phyllis," Sam comments. "I thought you might want to know about them."

Sam details what he has heard and Tom isn't surprised.

"Thank you for your candor," Tom says. "I assure you this is a fabrication of the truth."

Sam returns to his work area as Tom is left to ponder on what to do about this issue. He decides to approach his manager to discuss what has happened and how to employ damage control to get the situation under hand. It won't be easy, but this gossiper needs to be put out of business. They destroy both personal character and business productivity with their rumors.

Identifying

The dreams of the *Gossiper* are to have listening devices everywhere and walls with ears. They seek to collect as much information as possible on people and events so they will have topics for discussion. As you gaze on the sea of cubes in a corporation, you observe these individuals dashing down aisles gathering their information morsels. Uncovering *Gossipers* is an easy task. Key things to look for include:

- Sharing negative personal information about others
- Passion for discussing controversial company information
- Allowing work to pile up on their desk as they are out spreading their gossip
- Intently listening in on conversations hoping to learn topics for discussion
- Starting off conversations with "Did you hear about..." or "Let me tell you about..."
- Thriving on the misfortune of others and being excited to discuss it

If the *Gossiper* has been promoted to upper management, identification can be difficult. The true intent of their verbosity isn't without basis. Are they leaking information because there's a hidden agenda or are they trying to be malicious with internal company information and create a certain behavior or reaction out of employees?

Interaction

Consistent interaction with a *Gossiper* can be very unproductive for you. As demonstrated above, the *Gossiper* has a passion for controversies and disagreements that surface in the corporate environment. Be cautious, as the real conniving ones make a game out of stealing important information. They monitor office conversations and ask questions to flush out topics for discussion.

Some co-workers will establish a secret relationship with office *Gossipers,* hoping to obtain information that may prove to be useful. This is an unhealthy alliance and should be avoided at all costs. The information *Gossipers* hold has been modified to deliver the best effect to their audience. Trusting that details are accurate can place you at risk if the testimony is acted upon.

Deal with office *Gossipers* by avoiding them. Once someone has been identified a *Gossiper*, make an effort to abstain discussing anything remotely confidential near this personality. If they approach with a new rumor, politely but firmly inform them you have no interest in what they offer. Faced with a direct approach, *Gossiper* will move on to new prey.

Gossipers tend to seek out only those who are eager to hear the latest interoffice chat. They feed off the environment. If they are provided fuel, they will flourish.

If a *Gossiper* is spreading rumors about you in the office, confront this situation as soon as possible. The manner of approach should be professional but direct. Let them know exactly where your tolerance level is for office gossip.

From a benefit perspective, the *Gossiper* adds true value to the office environment when there is positive information to be shared. A new office promotion or changes in company policy are great examples of where the *Gossiper* will ensure the news is spread quickly.

Partners/Political Alliances

Gossipers will have very few partners or political alliances in the workplace—most corporate workers don't welcome them. With exceptions to upper management using the *Gossiper* as a channel to spread news, they will usually cause strife and mistrust in the office.

A *Gossiper* will try to partner up with a *Know-it-all*, *F.A.D.* ·or the *Spin-Doctor*. The *Know-it-all* and the *Spin-Doctor* are a source of information for the *Gossiper* while *F.A.D.* can share some of their fluff tactics. Yet, once the *Gossiper* shows their true colors, all three of the above personalities will make a 180-degree turn and sever any serious business ties. The biggest motivation for this change is a *Gossiper* will not bring much ROI (Return on Investment) to the relationship.

Long-term Effects

The *Gossiper* will continue to cause relational damage with co-workers if they don't re-evaluate and change behavior. Whether it's personal or company information, their desire to share such matters will alienate them. Promotions will be scarce, and job security questionable.

Gossipers will be doing the corporate environment a favor by keeping to themselves and refraining from sharing the irrelevant details about their colleagues.

The Armchair Manager
(Managing From Their Chair)

The Personality

Upper management sees the success of some employees with shaded glasses. Reality isn't as it appears, with these employees' success obtained through luck, market presence, or just showing up to take the order. Still, management rewards these individuals with promotions to join their ranks so these new managers can indoctrinate their workers and create contagious prosperity.

In their new positions these new managers' complacency and true characteristics take command. Their "just get by" attitude and a lack of leading by example has them working from their chair to guide their employees. They become so entangled in their new role that email, paperwork, and phone calls rule their day. They totally ignore what their employees need: hands-on training to show them the proper way to be successful. The new boss has become an *Armchair Manager*.

The Story

Digitron is going strong as they enter the third quarter of their financial year. They are nearing their most important time of the year: the fourth quarter, when a majority of annual sales are booked just before the holidays. It seems each customer wants an ample supply of digits on hand to start off the new year.

The Company has recently promoted Ralph—a new, brash, stellar sales person—to become the local business sales manager. His focus is to help drive third quarter business sales and build additional momentum heading into the busy fourth quarter.

He has won multiple awards in his previous job including rookie of the year, top sales person for the quarter—several times—sales person of the year, and team player of the year.

His success is the main reason for the promotion. Digitron is counting on his ability to apply this to his new team.

This is Ralph's first management position. Even though he has a proven sales track record in government sales, it will be a challenge to adapt to managing a team focused on corporate sales. The change to corporate sales brings an uncertainty to this proven salesperson. He has heard of the vicious corporate world of fast track sales. A small knot develops in his throat every time he thinks about this new position.

He is used to a long sales cycle, long-term customer relationships, and a slow arduous product design for the strict specifications the government requires. While in government sales, he spearheaded the sale of the ultra-camouflaged digit used in Bosnia and other military locations. Its discreet appearance and tough armor plating make it a military necessity and require high-density goo be used in its design.

Ralph has inherited a direct sales team of ten reps ranging from zero to four years of sales experience. Obviously, the real challenge for Ralph is to learn how to manage people who know more about corporate sales than he does.

"It shouldn't matter," he thinks. "A customer is a customer."

Phillip Thomas is one of the seasoned reps in the office and isn't particularly excited about Ralph's arrival due to his lack of corporate sales experience. He feels if a manager hasn't personally performed the job, then he can't respect them and doesn't believe there is much to learn from them either.

Jeremy, another member of the sales team, is the epitome of brand new—fresh out of college and a true greenhorn. He has to look twice to see if the customer is still breathing after he makes a sales call. There's a lot of development needed to bring his skills up to Digitron's minimal requirements. He doesn't prepare for sales calls by investigating the customers' businesses, position in their market, and competitors. Many times the customer knows more about the products that Jeremy is trying to sell than he does.

After three months on the job, Ralph begins to feel pressure from Digitron management regarding his team's lack of success. They have to sell more digits and with the holiday temps lined up waiting to be called in to help on the production lines, orders have to start flowing. "Order, build, and ship" is the Company motto. (There's even a Company song, but forget that. Ralph can't carry a tune if it was strapped to his back.)

Business hasn't turned around as aggressively as the management would like. Production from Phillip is getting the team by and is enough for Ralph to keep his job.

Another challenge Ralph's team is experiencing is a high attrition rate of more than thirty percent. There are two main reasons for this turnover. First, the reps don't seem happy and are finding other jobs. And second, Ralph is forced by management to move out reps that aren't performing. He doesn't know why they just can't sell.

Phillip frequently turns to him for assistance, but can't get his full attention during their one-on-one meetings.

"Ralph, I really need help with this customer issue," Phillip inquires. "The customer is frustrated with our performance on delivery. We keep missing ship dates and this is putting the customer in a bind to deliver to their customers."

"Hang on just a minute and let me finish this email," Ralph replies. "Okay, now I'm done. What was it that you needed?"

"I don't need anything," Phillip replies, frustrated by the lack of focus. "The customer wants to speak with you directly because we're behind in the delivery of our products."

"All I can say is I am your manager," Ralph proudly replies. "My job is to develop you as a sales person, so go ahead and figure out a solution and let me know what you come up with."

"Now why didn't I think of that?" Phillip muses silently. "Why doesn't that mossy-assed manager get out of his chair and help with this situation? "

Ralph continues to sit in his office and hammer out emails when he receives a call from Jeremy.

"Ralph!" Jeremy enthusiastically yells over the phone. "I just had a great appointment and the customer is interested in making a big purchase. He really likes what I shared with him about Digitron's products and services."

"That's great, Jeremy," Ralph says. "When will I have the order on my desk?"

Jeremy is a little confused because he doesn't really understand the corporate sales process or how his manager operates. Ralph's response is to be expected because he is unclear how the corporate sales process works himself. The government sales cycle took many years and he had a lot of help with his sales. This corporate stuff moves too fast, he thinks.

"Ralph, I could really use some help here," Jeremy pleads. "This was my first appointment and I really want to make sure we get the deal. What are my next steps?"

"I recommend checking our intranet Web page on the sales process," Ralph comments. "After you have done the research and met with the customer, let me know if you get the sale. I want you to know, Jeremy, that you're doing a great job. Go get 'em, tiger!"

Jeremy feels like he is being sent out into the jungle to take out a Bengal tiger with a fork. Maybe he could distract it and tickle it to death? He has no instructions. If he was armed with a gun, he believes he would be expected to shoot at anything that moves.

The following week Jeremy walks in with his head hanging down. Ralph looks up from his desk and sees this befuddled situation through his open door.

"Come on into my office, Jeremy. What's troubling you?" Ralph asks. "Why such the long face today?"

"I just lost that big deal I was working on," Jeremy replies. "Boy, was I unprepared. The customer knew more about our products and about sales than I did. I could have really used some help."

"That's okay," Ralph says. "Sounds like you gave it a great effort." He stretches with great effort on his part to pat Jeremy on the back without having to remove his gluteus maximus from the chair.

"You'll get it next time," Ralph believes himself as he encourages Jeremy.

Ralph returns to his emails. Jeremy is standing in front of a true *Armchair Manager*. Jeremy turns and walks out of the office to the sound of typing on a computer keyboard.

Ralph sometimes wonders if he sits in a chair too long would his butt fuse to it. Oh well, too much to do to worry about that.

Identifying

The lives of *Armchair Managers* revolve around their chairs. Their day is spent living, eating, and working at their desk with hardly a moment spent out of their seat.

Key ingredients to identifying this manager are:

- Lives in office chair
- Provides vague answers to questions that may require rising from chair
- Spends majority of time on email, phone, and seated conversations in chair
- Delegates managerial responsibility to a team leader in order to continue with emails and phone calls dealt with in chair
- Rarely visits customers (external or internal)
- Is preoccupied with emails during team or one-on-one meetings

Interaction

Working successfully with an *Armchair Manager* in the corporate environment is realistic. They traditionally don't like confrontation. An irrational approach for requesting assistance from them will result in quickly being directed to another source for the information. You should take a persistent, but professional, approach of interaction to obtain the desired information from them. If all attempts to recruit support from the *Armchair Manager* fail, you should then turn to your co-workers for help.

A recommended approach to working successfully with this personality is to try to come up with your own ideas or solutions to existing situations or problems. All of this information should be presented to the manager for their input, direction, and final blessing. The goal is to try to bring a solution instead of throwing another problem on their plate. This may help in working to avoid conflict, but be cautious.

This approach may lead to a common response of "I'm not sure," or "You'll be able to find the answer in our 3,000-page Company handbook." (Which, by the way, has no index.)

From a productivity standpoint, the *Armchair Manager* brings the strength of email proficiency and an organized desk.

Partners/Political Alliances

Armchair Managers don't associate with anyone who can threaten their existence. They will align with other *Armchair Managers, Retired on the Job*, the *Gluteus Maximizer, F.A.D., Ascendo Inabilitus*, and possibly the *Spin-Doctor*. These corporate personalities all show case-similar characteristics. This includes delegation of work and resources, spin, fluff, and diversion of support.

They will avoid personalities such as *Napoleon* and the *Sour Puss*. These personality types will confront the *Armchair Manager*. They will not accept the half-truths or lack of attention to details, which causes frustration through lack of productivity.

Long-term Effects

Over time, *Armchair Managers* will survive in their positions if their team is strong enough to keep production up. This will ensure job security. The caveat with high producers is they can be high maintenance, thus requiring this personality to assist. Even if their assistance is vague, this won't be enough to *unseat* the *Armchair Manager*.

This personality is measured by and accountable for true team results. If disgruntled employee issues continually surface and can't be resolved, management may take a close look at this team. The *Armchair Manager's* team will need a history of success for this personality to avoid dismissal or reassignment.

If I told you Not to jump off the Empire State Building, would you?

Yeah, I probably would.

Get your butt home.

XXX

The Ostrich
(Working in Their Own Space)

The Personality

Unlike the myth that ostriches bury their heads in the sand, corporate *Ostriches* actually do bury their heads in their work. There are several causes for this retreat from society as *Ostriches* work alone in their preferred reclusive state.

Personality can lead to this withdrawal from the loud, hustle and bustle of corporate life. Another cause is being caught up in a rally where the *Ostrich* is the object of the game. These situations don't sit well with them and they retreat to more comfortable ground.

The Story

Betty—who just transferred to Digitron's West Coast office to take over as a compliance manager—has been with the Company for three years. She sets high goals for herself and strives to do her best at everything she does. With her thin, tall frame and pleasant demeanor, she has no trouble in getting anyone to talk with her. People gravitate towards her as if she has a magical force. Her first order of business is to get to know everyone and their respective responsibilities so she can work more effectively with her co-workers. Her job requires investigating all procedural details and ensuring the office meets the rigid standards Corporate sets.

Betty meets Buster who has been with the Company in the same position at the same office for fourteen years. He is slightly overweight with disheveled brown hair and dress. Being shy and reserved, he doesn't interact well with others. Betty observes he keeps to himself and speaks quietly. Buster never laughs or speaks up in a group, she is told. From her observations and input from her co-workers, she recognizes this personality—it's the *Ostrich*—and she has seen them hide exclusively at Corporate.

At Corporate there are camouflaged herds of *Ostriches* everywhere, though a person can walk the halls and never see one. They hide from the world in their cubes. It practically takes a crow bar to get them to come out and attend meetings or group lunches—areas outside their comfort space.

Betty considers what she has learned about the *Ostrich* and realizes they have their head in their work and are clueless how the corporate world outside their work functions. They are totally unaware of their surroundings and really don't care. This reminds Betty of a quote from the movie *National Lampoon's Christmas Vacation:* "You couldn't hear a dump truck driving through a nitroglycerin plant."

Many ask, "Why is the *Ostrich* that way?" There can be several reasons. The first is they may not care much about others since they are wrapped up in their world and are, actually, introverts. Others have lower priority. The main focus is on what they are working on. Shyness is probably what has caused this situation.

Another reason could be that they have been burned in the past helping and working with others, so their desire is to avoid being treated poorly again. This bad experience may have involved a personality clash, an unjust imbalance in workload, or credit was taken for their work.

Betty imagines a group working together on a project where Buster is assigned a section of the project to research and report his findings. He retreats to gather information, completes his assignment, and reluctantly returns to meet with the group to present his findings. Because the *Ostrich* is uncomfortable presenting in meetings, they muddle through their presentations and hastily return to seclusion.

Betty wonders how the *Ostrich* sees the world from their eyes. Most likely they see crazed people running around trying to jockey for social acceptance—Suzie running to the bathroom every ten minutes to see if her hair still looks good; Bob running around patting that baby of a belly. "When are you going to have that baby?" Betty hears people asking Bob all the time.

Betty decides it's best to get to know the *Ostrich*. Rather than force Buster to work in her world, she will meet him on his own ground. She will have lunch with him in a non-threatening environment.

It's 11:30 a.m. on Friday. Betty walks over to Buster's cube where he is hard at work entering numbers on a spreadsheet.

"Hello, Buster," Betty exclaims. "How are you today?"

"Fine," he replies as he glances up from his work.

"I'm new here and really want to have a nice lunch today," she comments. "Could you suggest a place nearby?"

"I like McNeal's just down the street," he quietly answers.

"You know, I hate to eat alone," she says. "Will you join me? It's my treat."

This gets Buster's attention as he lays his pencil down and looks directly at Betty.

"Okay," he says.

Buster feels Betty is non-threatening and a free lunch is always welcome on his budget. They drive to lunch in Betty's car. Buster explains his usual routine when visiting this establishment. He loves this little sandwich shop where he picks up his lunch and brings it back to his desk, or eats in his car parked in a nice shady spot. He hates to eat alone, but finds solitude with his required safe haven. Betty is relaxed and non-threatening in her discussion with him.

She convinces Buster to dine on the patio so perhaps a little sunshine may permeate that milky white skin of his. Vampires have better tans, she imagines. During lunch, Betty's wants to get to know Buster better, learn what makes him tick, and determine how valuable an information resource he is. From their discussions she sees a tremendous amount of knowledge being harbored in a remote cube in the office. Most people in the office take Buster at face value: a quiet, meek person who does his work and leaves everyone alone.

As they start their lunch, Bob drives up and orders two sandwiches to go from the outside take out window. He also picks up some snacks, a large drink and some desserts. With an armload of calories, he heads back to his car and is off in a cloud of exhaust smoke to scarf all those goodies down somewhere else.

Seeing Bob causes Betty's mind to wander for a moment. She has heard rumors of Bob's meals. If anyone breaks the feeding plane within two feet of his lunch, they may be bitten or even worse, wounded with a flying utensil. She remembers this and takes caution whenever she is around him in the break room.

She snaps out of her mental state and returns to lunch. The two discuss office politics and Buster's background in between bites of their delicious sandwiches. Betty realizes he knows a lot more than what others give him credit for. While others are socializing at the coffee station, Buster is spending his time learning more about Digitron's systems and has become quite an expert in several areas.

She shares with Buster the details of her new job and her requirement to write up many reports. She welcomes Buster's input. He has a significant amount of knowledge and this would lend nicely to enhance her reports. They finish their lunch and head back to the salt mine. Buster thanks Betty for the nice gesture. He will consider contributing to her reports.

As she settles in her workplace, Betty thinks about her lunch conversation with Buster. She detects someone has burned him in the past. After a little investigation, she discovers Bob once offered to trade Buster a "snack pack" if Buster would help him on a report he was doing. Buster came through with his end, but arrived too late into the lunch hour as Bob had already "wolfed" down the treat. Never leave any food lingering around Bob is the moral to that story. Buster was not happy about the outcome and retreated to his cube amidst office laughter.

Betty wants to make sure Buster feels he will receive ample reward for his input. Rather than make this a promise in words, she decides to put it in writing. She drafts an outline of her reports, submits it to management, and notes Buster as a valuable resource whose services can enhance these reports. She makes sure Buster receives a copy of the recognition.

After being recognized, Buster is convinced all Betty has spoken about is truthful. He starts to open up and contribute to her reports. He has come across all sorts of personality types trying to take advantage of him—*High Promise, No Delivery, F.A.D.,* the *Napoleon, Ascendo Inabilitus,* the list goes on. Betty seems to be honest and he is committed to working with her as he sees this as a positive work relationship, one that doesn't occur every day.

Identifying

In the corporate plains, the *Ostrich* runs free from strife and heated arguments. But where are they? Even though they are known to exist, rarely are they seen. Learning to recognize this special species of the corporate personality family is key to working with them. Their traits are:

- Selecting a remote office area to work
- Staying in their office area unless they have to attend a meeting
- Rarely initiating interaction unless necessary
- Busy working and learning at the workstations while others participate in intra-office socialization
- Successfully becoming a wallflower by being reluctant to speak up in groups
- Adopting a quiet, low key personality and behavior
- Being detail-oriented and a knowledge specialist

Interaction

The *Ostrich* is a quiet, almost hidden personality within the corporate world. They prefer their solitude and require others to respect it. Even though they are not a hostile personality, they can withdraw further if not approached carefully.

If you can create a comfortable environment to get to know this personality, then you will have an opportunity for a successful working relationship. Forcing *Ostriches* to work with you or positioning them in an uncomfortable environment will result in this personality retreating even further into their work. Your best bet is to get to know them and take it slow so they know there is honest intent and no games are being played.

The best way to break down any barriers is to find out what *Ostriches* like. Do they take breaks to smoke or drink coffee? Do they like to eat a special food or at a particular place? Interaction during these leisure times creates a safer environment to get to know them.

Even though Buster smokes, Betty doesn't. Her uncle died of the black lung disease after working just one day in a coal mine. This makes her think twice about anything that could harm her lungs.

Taking great care to avoid threatening or uncomfortable situations is extremely important—especially when initial contact is made and trust is being built. Being in uncomfortable situations before makes them gun shy. The old saying "Fool me once, shame on you; fool me twice, shame on me," comes into play. They won't let themselves be caught up in this situation again and it's extremely hard to rebuild trust once it's broken.

The *Ostrich* is very knowledgeable and this information is valuable to the organization. Instead of spending time socializing, they learn and retain company knowledge. It's important for you to be aware of their feelings and comfort level. Adjust a situation so they will be more comfortable and this will work to your advantage. Next time you need to interact with an *Ostrich* personality, they will be more open to work with you and help those around them.

Partners/Political Alliances

The *Ostrich* has very few political alliances. They may align with other *Ostriches* or with those they feel very comfortable with. The alliance isn't for political reasons; it's for comfort and social reasons. As mentioned above, they are introverts; thus they aren't proactive in seeking out friendships. It's when others come to them and make the experience comfortable they feel compelled to create an alliance.

Long-term Effects

Over time *Ostriches* find themselves stuck in their current position. When others are vying for promotions and opportunities, *Ostriches* are in their corners constantly working. Only when there is a manager or co-worker who recognizes the *Ostrich's* diligence or an opening is created through attrition or expansion will a promotion be afforded. The *Ostrich* usually doesn't pursue promotions and higher responsibilities with the same passion of other corporate personalities.

The CYA
(Cover Your Assets)

The Personality

Paranoia can run rampant in the work environment. Those seeking total protection against all possible threats work hard to strengthen defenses to repel all avenues of attack. Resembling a military operation, they reinforce garrisons, stockpile ammunition, and rejuvenate alliances. Nothing is overlooked as the campaign is indefinitely in full swing and this individual becomes a *CYA*.

Those working with or for this person are wading knee deep in paper, reports, emails, and meetings as nothing is overlooked for assurance against a threat. *F.A.D.'s* are challenged in tree destruction as the *CYA* continues a self-imposed crusade of personal protection.

The Story

Herbert has been a sales manager in the central branch of Digitron for six years. He loves his job and helping people. His hefty build and thinning hair have others believing he dedicates himself totally to work. (All this worry about his job doesn't help the hair situation one bit.) Peers and employees have noticed he is becoming jittery and has amassed a nice data storage facility in his small office. There are filing and CD storage cabinets everywhere as visitors try to squeeze into what little space remains. Herbert considers himself a fair person and reviews a situation before making a decision. But the Corporation is undergoing some changes, causing added stress in Herbert's work life. He's overly cautious in everything he does.

Management is rolling out the new Hindenburg product line and policies dealing with ethics and proper accounting practices are flooding Herbert's email in-box. With the staff reorganizing in the field as well, being adaptive is key to surviving and retaining mental cognizance. Everyone has to maintain a level head and know the confusion associated with change is temporary until glitches are worked out and everyone learns the new details.

These changes have an exaggerated effect on Herbert, which actually scares him. He's comfortable with the old environment and although changes are good, everything is in flux—new products, new policies and a heightened awareness from corporate. He is overwhelmed with confusion, training, and cultural changes within the workplace.

Susan—from the West Coast office—is on loan for a special project to oversee a sales automation implementation and will stay for two to three months to ensure the project is completed. She helped launch this project in her West Coast branch and things were very successful.

Herbert's paranoid about Susan's presence during such a tumultuous time. Combine the internal changes the Corporation is enduring with the corporate investigations in the news, Herbert can easily justify to himself why he has such an uncertain attitude. Digitron is overly precautious in ensuring it doesn't make any *faux pas*.

As Susan starts implementing the project, Herbert becomes increasingly worried something will go wrong and he will be involved. With the new Corporate environment providing a little nudge, Herbert has become a full-fledged *CYA*. His staff has always thought of him as a little peculiar, but now every time someone requests support, he asks for the request in writing and saves it in triplicate. The original is saved in an off-line folder on the hard drive with backups on CD and a shared drive.

"It never hurts to plan for the worst," he thinks. "Could you email me that request?" he asks one of his staff.

This will ensure he has everything documented. Herbert addresses his staff only in writing so there won't be any misinterpretation of his orders and direction.

Now that Susan is around, he knows Corporate is watching her. Therefore, they are watching him. All operations must go smoothly and his paranoia has him constantly looking over his shoulder. He thinks of a story from a Vietnam vet he knows. That man is so paranoid he mounted a mirror on the wall in front of his desk so no one could sneak up on him. Perhaps Herbert should order some mirrors?

Susan notices Herbert is very edgy and is always looking to cover things up. When she asked for a report on last week's sales, he stammered and finally replied he was still working on it. Susan could tell he was hiding something by his nervousness and voice inflection. She recognizes a *CYA* when she sees one.

She has known several *CYAs* in her day—some are tame and others are more extreme. They can hardly function with all the bureaucracy they create to cover themselves for an emergency. The amount of paperwork in their drive to document everything is staggering. It drives those who want to get their job done efficiently crazy.

After asking a few questions and a simple observation, Susan notices Herbert has his staff completing numerous reports on their sales, prospects, leads, and weekly schedule. They are probably doing reports on their reports. Trees are probably scared when they hear Herbert's name mentioned.

The staff is going crazy with all this reporting and Herbert is worse than ever. They knew he is a little nutty with his requests, but now he is going way overboard. Even his staff realizes he is a *CYA*.

Everyone sees what Herbert is doing and what he has become with his overwhelming paranoia. Next he will probably want to mount shoplifting mirrors all around the office. It feels like big brother is watching and you had better mind yourself or else.

Herbert senses the troops are restless. He hears an increasing amount of complaints from them and spends additional time counseling and coaching them through their issues. One will have questions on one of Herbert's required reports while another is attempting to justify why she doesn't have time to process all the paperwork now required. Something has to be done because too much of his day is spent reacting rather than managing sales.

Several members of the sales staff decide to have lunch and discuss Herbert's changes and how unbearable things have become. It seems their day is spent doing reports, reading and replying to emails, and attending numerous meetings Herbert holds each week. When is there time to sell? Upper management is pushing for sales. They don't care that salespeople have to spend part of their day doing reports. The sales department is responsible for sales, and management is going to hold them accountable.

One member, Paul, speaks up and takes the lead with the group.

"In order to do our jobs properly, there has to be balance," he states. "Reports are needed to track and detail certain aspects of sales, but there has to be a limit. Too many reports will take the focus off the desired result—sales."

It's decided the group will draft a detailed report—perhaps it could be called a "study" to make people feel better about it—highlighting the details of each report they are required to complete by Herbert. In addition, the data source, duplication of information, and the time required to complete each of Herbert's reports is noted. Each group member works independently on this assignment and they plan to reconvene and discuss the findings.

In the meantime, Paul checks with his peers in other groups across the country to see if they are required to submit the same type reports. Do other groups reporting to Herbert's director—Timmy—have to do these reports? Paul is looking for consistency among the groups. Just how much of this over-reporting is simply Herbert's paranoia?

When the group reconvenes, they find 60% of the data is redundant and 45% of their week is spent filling out reports just for Herbert's review. In addition, they detail what's important to the department and of course it's sales—profitable sales. Money. Cashola. The green! These are the responses from the group.

Profitable sales have to lead to positive results and there are many theories within the Company on how to get there. Some think if they let sales happen they will come. Others believe in micro management combined with reps saddled with reports to keep the wild beasts under control. Balance between moderate reporting and ample time to perform the job is another perspective.

After all, if reports are what they want, they could hire a room full of *F.A.D.s.* Mount Saint Helen's damage to forests won't even touch the tree destruction a group of these people could accomplish.

They complete the report and present it to Herbert with Paul being the elected speaker. Herbert nearly blows a bowel, feeling his management methods are being challenged. Changes like this could get a person fired with the turmoil going on in this Company. No waves are the common mode of operation these days. No-wave Herbert tries to dispute the data and findings from Paul to no avail. The facts are in black and white.

Paul can tell he isn't getting anywhere with Herbert—it's a futile and frustrating experience. There's no point in continuing to bang his head against a brick wall so it's time for plan B. He believes the ideal strategy is to contact Timmy, the department director and present the findings to him. It will be necessary to show the Return on Investment—ROI—and the impact of the reports on the group and their production.

After calling Timmy and obtaining his agreement to review, Paul emails the report to him. He also includes several times to be chosen for a conference call to review the information.

Timmy—located in the Nome, Alaska plant—receives the email and reviews its contents. He considers a best time for the two to talk and replies to Paul.

The agreed meeting time arrives and at 3:00 p.m., the two are in conference to discuss the report. Paul reviews each point, emphasizes the ROI, and notes the enormous amount of money the Company is spending on salespeople to generate reports. He points out the dramatic difference in sales performance before Herbert became paranoid and the current level. Herbert's acting like a full-fledged, basket case *CYA*. Paul didn't put it in exactly those words, but he did get his point across.

He highlights the effects of lost sales in both Company revenue and salesperson commissions. The fact is many of the salespeople are looking for other jobs.

"Are these results worth the tons of reports generated and lying around?" Paul asks.

Paul concludes with detailing the amount of time necessary to train sales replacements brought in as the result of the anticipated attrition.

Timmy is impressed and comments Paul has done a thorough job.

"You and your team have done a great job, Paul," he replies. "I have a few more questions for you."

Paul fields the questions with confidence and Timmy thanks him again for the team's hard work.

"The Company appreciates initiative taken to watch out for its best interest. Please thank all the team members for me."

They conclude the call and Timmy is left to consider how to handle this situation. He's convinced things have to change and the only way to do this is to have a discussion with Herbert. He decides to telephone him and cover the points discussed during his call with Paul.

"Herbert, this is Timmy. How are you?"

Herbert is shaking from nervousness.

"Why am I getting a call from the director?" he thinks. "I'm fine, sir," he replies.

"I apologize for the poor phone quality," Timmy comments. "There's nothing we can do about it." The crackling on the line sometimes happens during the moose-mating season in Alaska. Timmy doesn't care to elaborate.

Timmy comments on the extreme loss of productivity in Herbert's department and how it appears he has become a report hog. He has to bite his tongue about another issue with Herbert. It seems that Herbert is packing on the pounds as well and is becoming a full-fledged scarf hound in constant action.

Herbert starts to choke and places the phone down for a moment to get a class of water. This gives Timmy a chance for his mind to wander and reflect on a theory about weight he has heard. The world maintains a constant weight and as one person loses weight, another gains. This weight transfer is caused by the release of free fat electrons from the person shedding tonnage that attach themselves to another pour soul, thus they gain weight. The office is running scared and busy, so someone must be losing weight while Herbert attracts all the free fat electrons.

Herbert returns and picks up the receiver with his throat cleared. Timmy elaborates on the true intent of the call, which is sales.

"Clean it up," he says to Herbert. "Quit being a *CYA* and so paranoid. Manage the team and encourage activity and forget all the report activity. Get in the field and help your people."

Herbert takes a deep breath and replies.

"Yes sir. I will get things under control."

"Good," Timmy replies and hangs up the phone.

Herbert makes adjustments on the amount of reports his team is responsible for. Sales are on the up tick and morale is improving. Now entire forests can breathe a sigh of relief.

Identifying

At first glance, the *CYA* may appear to be a *Micro Manager*. The main difference between these two personalities is the intent. *CYAs* manage with paranoia to protect themselves while *Micro Managers* believe their staff needs to be scrutinized for every detail or they will never amount to anything. For you to identify *CYAs*, it's necessary to consider some of their characteristics. These include:

- Paranoia
- Constant paper trail of all actions
- Multiple backups of documentation
- Excessive reports and projects – if they are a manager
- Meticulous storage habits as all work is archived for future reference
- Workplace challenge—co-workers (staff if CYA is manager) find them difficult to deal with

Just as everyone working with Herbert can see he is a *CYA*, you too will discover how to identify this paranoid personality in the workplace.

Interaction

It's best not to challenge a *CYA*. Due to their paranoid state, reactions can be varied. Approach them and present reasonable facts to show how to achieve productivity improvement.

The *CYA* can be a co-worker, manager, or customer. Although each of these individuals view threats to their position in a similar manner, they react in different ways. The co-worker defends their position by collecting documentation and encouraging those who interact with them to respect and conform to their work style. The manager invokes their documentation requirements on their staff to ensure all interaction is properly accounted for. The customer demands all communication be recorded for future reference and measurement. For you to have success in working with any one of these *CYA* types, listen, acknowledge, and respond.

If the *CYA* won't accept the information offered, back off and take another course of action. Collect the facts and present to higher management for their support.

Partners/Political Alliances

CYAs have close affiliation with each other. They compare their paranoia and work style to better prepare for any threats they could encounter. It's their way of building better internal alliances. It ensures they are doing all they can from a documentation perspective to protect them from anything that could harm their corporate existence.

Other groups such as *Gluteus Maximizers* and *Ascendo Inabilituses* will associate themselves with *CYA's*. They are looking to climb the corporate food chain and urge the *CYA* to assist in protection advice, sponsorship, and a good word to management about them. *CYAs* are looking for support, so these groups find solace in each other.

It's questionable whether *Napoleons* and other figureheads will appreciate *CYAs*. If the paranoia is too extreme, this personality becomes a paper pusher so their inefficiency is useless to this power ruler. Otherwise, the monarchy will examine this personality's possible contribution.

From a contributory standpoint, result-oriented *CYAs* add benefit to a company from a documentation and work output perspective. Data is available for company examination in addition to work completion.

Long-term Effects

CYAs limit themselves on advancement. The extremists spend so much time trying to cover their assets, they don't have time to perform their job correctly.

Those who work for a *CYA*—unless they are one also—find it a frustrating experience. This leads to both internal and external complaints. Should these complaints continue to an unacceptable level, the *CYA* will be managed out of a job or into a new department.

Let the Games End

It's our hope you now have deeper insight into, and a more thorough understanding of, the many personalities you can face in the corporate arena. Additionally, we hope the work has empowered you with the skills and knowledge to work successfully with these unique personalities. This work has addressed only some of the corporate personalities in the corporate world who continue to play their games. Today's corporate world is challenging enough; take heed and do your part in ending the games.

We are also confident you found this book light-hearted and enlightening with a look into the many corporate personalities you may not have been aware of. Use this book as a continued reference to assist you in recognizing challenging corporate personalities and developing your career. When armed with the know-how found in **Corporate Games**, you can identify and interact with these personalities. You'll also understand the partners, political alliances, and long-term effects of each of these corporate personalities. Because of the deeper under-standing gained from this reading, you will be able to better avoid corporate games and even stop them.

As you can attest from the adjacent illustration and the readings with their respective illustrations, the *Corporate Mutt's* true identity has been revealed. Now you can see this complex breed's actual character as a blending of these per-sonalities. Although our interpretation of this mongrel is a powerful ruler combined with a hidden agenda and a workaholic, keep an open mind in the corporate world. Any combination of personalities can form to create this breed.

Good luck with your current and future career growth in today's corporate environment!

Appendix I

Corporate Personalities

The Armchair Manager: This personality manages from their chair. They rarely move about, leaving their team to survive and hopefully succeed on their own. They have a very hands-off management style and their office closely resembles their home.

Ascendo Inabilitus: These employees work at a level of incompetency. They have been promoted to a state of ineffectiveness and are struggling to survive. Be cautious in dealing with them.

The Backstabber: Takes credit for others' work when possible to cover up their inabilities and to promote their well-being. Uncover by listening and networking with others in the office to help identify. Document all of your work when interacting with this personality. Make sure management is aware of your capabilities and contributions.

The Best of Breed: This unique corporate personality ensures they are the best in their department. If they are a manager, they seek individuals who are inferior so they appear overwhelmingly superior.

Corporate Gumbo: This is the unique language of the *Corporate Mutt*. Examples of this are spin, fluff, micro management, etc.

The Corporate Ladder: This success seeker stops at nothing to get ahead. They imagine others with rungs on their backs to help them get a little further up the corporate ladder.

The Corporate Mutt: A combination of corporate personalities. Just as some dogs are made up of several breeds and are called mutts, the *Corporate Mutt* is made up of several corporate personalities. Sometimes a dominant personality will surface and individuals can be more accurately identified.

The Corporate Player: Holds to the corporate line at all costs. Their motto is: "If it's not in the company handbook or guidelines, then it must not be important." They don't believe in thinking outside of the box. Interaction is difficult since they are unwilling to look at the big picture.

The Court Adviser: They create their own mini-empire by working through an authority figure. They lend advice on improvements and changes and watch as their words turn into reality. This unique positioning provides the *Court Adviser* authority without responsibility.

The Cover Up: This individual works hard to cover up their job performance. They seek protection from a larger group called *The Untouchables*. Be cautious in working with this personality, as their substance is lacking and priorities are personal. Backlash is venomous when challenged.

The CYA: This corporate personality seeks to cover their assets. To prepare for any assault on their job, they ensure there is a healthy paper trail to back up their word. Many times those who work with or for this individual suffer through long processes and mountains of paperwork.

Exploiting Talents: They utilize any talent they have to obtain success. Their strong networking skills coupled with flirting help build key alliances with upper management. Because of their powerful alliances and corporate sponsors, don't cross them.

F.A.D.: This corporate personality substitutes fluff for facts that makes it difficult to believe anything they say. In addition, their administrative nature is recreating every document to accentuate their personal touch. And lastly, their passion to delegate has co-workers hiding in their cubes in fear of being recruited to do *F.A.D.'s* work. Avoid this individual if you can, as they will only bog you down and keep you from your own work.

Gluteus Maximizer: They focus their efforts on smooching to obtain benefits. This is to get ahead or cover up their lack of abilities and drive to perform their work. They accomplish these feats by overcompensating with compliments and puckering up to management or whomever will assist in their career.

The Gossiper: This individual's passion is spreading rumors about individuals and the company they work for. They thrive on "insider" information. Be polite yet firm when interacting with this personality. This will communicate to them you are not interested in their work.

Hidden Agendas: Their agenda is secret and violates company initiatives. When you are in play within their game, it's up to you to figure out their hidden agenda. Request written confirmation of what they want you to accomplish and secure *Hidden Agenda's* stamp of approval.

High Promise, No Delivery: This corporate personality challenges those who don't help to fulfill their promises. They over-promise a product or service without consideration of processes and procedures. Others have to scramble to keep the good word of the company intact. They have a tendency to blame others for their lack of integrity.

The Information Hog: Hoards information for job security. Get to know them and earn their trust. Open an avenue of information sharing by contributing valuable details they seek to increase their knowledge.

The Know-it-all: They attempt to learn all and are passionate about sharing this knowledge with everyone. Frequent statements are: "Yes, I have done that" or "Let me tell you more about... ". Be assertive and direct to limit their interference.

The Micro Manager: They scrutinize every detail of their employees. No rock goes unturned as this infinitesimal detail-oriented individual drives their employees crazy with excessive reporting, meetings and conference calls. The best way to handle is to satisfy their requests and you will see their demands dwindle. Management of under performers to overachieve is a positive of this personality.

The Napoleon: Creates their own empire. The *Napoleon* manages and directs operations their way, while modifying the corporate directive to make their self-created kingdom prosper. They hold great power and authority. Harsh punishment can be administered to those who don't conform to this individual's directive. They are very assertive and accomplish a tremendous amount of work.

The Ostrich: The *Ostrich* works in his or her own private space away from others. They seek tranquility and isolation from the busyness of the work environment, because it's overwhelming for them. Past work experience has caused them to become an introvert or gun shy for fear of being burned again in a company game. They are friendly to work with once they find trust in those who seek their assistance.

Retired on the Job: Does as little as possible to maintain job security. This person is unmotivated. Needs to be shown positives in doing their job properly for them to actively contribute.

The Sour Puss: This individual is just plain grumpy. Something happened to them either professionally or personally and they gripe about everything. Work with them carefully as association with their dynamics can create a negative perception for you.

The Spin-Doctor: They attempt to turn negatives into positives. Realize *Spin-Doctors* are those who specialize in convincing others change is always a good thing. Request the truth and temper "the *Doctor's*" spin with reality.

The Untouchables: An unproductive and inefficient organization surviving through sponsorship of an authority figure. Questioning this groups lack of productivity is met with a harsh reprisals and support from their sponsor. Work around these people whenever possible and directly with them carefully to avoid confrontation.

The Workaholic: There is too much work to do and not enough time to do it. They are driven towards productivity with minimal social and family time. The level of influence on co-workers is dependent on this individual's status in the organization—manager or worker. They are similar to a worker bee and have very little downtime. Can be highly productive and efficient.

Appendix II

Movie	Release Date	Studio
American Pie	1999	MGM
Animal House	1978	Universal Studios
Armed and Dangerous	1986	Columbia Tri-Star
Back to the Future	1985	Universal Studios
Back to School	1986	MGM
Billy Madison	1995	MCA
Blast From the Past	1999	New Line Cinemas
Clueless	1995	Paramount Pictures
Doc Hollywood	1991	Warner Bros.
The Family Man	2000	Universal Studios
Ferris Bueller's Day Off	1986	Paramount Pictures
Fletch	1985	Universal Studios
Funny Farm	1988	Warner Bros.
Glengarry Glen Ross	1992	New Line Cinemas
I'm No Angel	1933	Paramount Pictures
Jerry Maguire	1996	Columbia Tri-Star
The Mask	1994	New Line Cinemas
Major Payne	1995	MCA
Me, Myself and Irene	2000	20th Century Fox
Meet the Parents	2000	Universal Studios

Movie	Release Date	Studio
Miss Congeniality	2000	Warner Bros.
My Blue Heaven	1990	Warner Bros.
National Lampoon's Christmas Vacation	1989	Warner Bros.
The Nutty Professor	1996	Universal Studios
Office Space	1999	20th Century Fox
Princess Bride	1987	MGM
Road Trip	2000	Dreamworks Skg
Superman II	1980	Warner Bros.
Trading Places	1983	Paramount Pictures
Used Cars	1980	Columbia Tri-Star
Wall Street	1987	20th Century Fox
XXX	2002	Columbia Tri-Star
Zoolander	2001	Paramount Pictures

Other References

Name	Release	Author/Studio
English Fairy Tales	1898	David Nutt
Huey Lewis & The News Fore!	1986	Chrysalis
ID 10 T Error		pseudodictionary.com
Rodney Dangerfield	various	Rodney Dangerfield
Saturday Night Live	1975- present	NBC
Star Trek, the Next Generation	1989	Paramount Pictures

Glossary

agua Spanish for water.

Alec Baldwin Popular actor starring in movies such as *Glengarry Glen Ross.*

alpaca Domesticated South American mammal. Similar to a llama. Becoming popular to breed and sell in U.S.

baño Spanish for bathroom.

Bengal tiger Large wild cat found in Asia.

Better Business Bureau Organization A private organization who's goal is to promote and foster the highest ethical relationship between businesses and the public through voluntary self-regulation, consumer and business education, and service excellence.

çe la vie French for "Oh, well."

charlatan A fraud who claims to have knowledge and skill they don't have.

cloaked Camouflaged or hidden.

Corporate Gumbo Language of the Corporate Mutt. Usually spin, fluff, etc.

Corporate Mutt Combination of multiple corporate personalities.

Cubans Cigar imported from the country of Cuba.

digit Fictitious general product line manufactured and sold by Digitron.

digit sprocket Fictitious specific digit manufactured and sold by Digitron.

Digitron Fictitious company created for ***Corporate Games*** book.

Datsun Japanese automobile made by Nissan, which dates back to 1911.

entomologist A zoologist that studies insects.

faux pas A social blunder or false step.

fiefdom Anything under an individual's complete control.

filleted To slice or cut.

flux capacitor Fictional power source in movie *Back to the Future.*

Georgia Pacific Company founded in 1927 as a hardwood lumber wholesaler. Through expansion and acquisitions has grown to become one of the world's leading manufacturers and distributors of building products, packaging, paper, pulp and related chemicals and tissue. Headquartered in Atlanta, Georgia-Pacific employs more than 75,000 people at some 600 locations worldwide.

governor(s) A mechanical device for controlling (restricting) the speed of an engine.

greenhorn New hire entering workforce who can be easily deceived.

Hindenburg German air blimp that crashed in New Jersey in 1937.

Holy Grail Considered to be the cup from which Christ drank from at the Last Supper.

Hyundai Korean automobile manufacturing company.

HQ Head Quarters.

inscribe To place in writing.

IRS Internal Revenue Service

IT Department Information Technology Department which is a fancy name for data processing.

Leavenworth Area within Kansas where four prison complexes exist.

Lumbergh Character in the movie *Office Space*.

Malcolm Baldridge A former Secretary of Commerce of the United States. An award is named after this individual presented by the President of the United to large and small manufacturing and service businesses as well as education and health care organizations who excel in leadership, strategic planning, information and analysis, customer and market focus, human resource focus, process management, and business results.

Mars Lander NASA unmanned space craft used to survey planet Mars.

MO Mode of operation.

Mogen David A New York kosher winery.

Monet Claude Monet, 18th century impressionist painter.

Montezuma's Revenge Montezuma was an Aztec ruler who disappeared at the time of the Spanish conquest of Mexico. Revenge involves afflicting visitors who drink unfiltered water and food they aren't used to with infestation of the intestines. Such is the cost of colonization.

nitroglycerin A colorless, oily, toxic liquid used to make a powerful explosive and an important ingredient in most forms of dynamite.

nauga-hide Fictitious animal whose hide is used for leather substitute. Actual product is naugahyde, a vinyl-coated fabric used as an artificial leather.

Pony Express Postal service in 18th century western United States. Mail was carried via horseback in relay fashion to expedite delivery.

PR Public Relations. Section of a company that deals with general public through publicity.

ROI Return on Investment.

serf Medieval tenant farmer who paid a percentage of crops as rent and owed a number of other obligations to a landlord.

sovereign Chief of state in a monarchy.

Twinkie Snack food made by the Hostess Corporation.

waders Waterproof overalls with attached boots.

Weyerhaeuser World's largest producer of softwood and hardwood lumber. Products include lumber, plywood, oriented strand board, engineered wood, chemical wood pulp, coated and uncoated papers, and containerboard. Headquartered in Federal Way, Washington.

win-win Mutually beneficial partnership and outcome.

Index

Cool River Publishing
Quick Order Form

WEB www.coolriverpub.com
PHONE 719.487.1827 or 800.338.3892   FAX 719.487.1767
POSTAL ORDERS
Cool River Publishing, Alan Hirschfeld
590 Highway 105 #301 • Monument, CO 80132 USA

Please send _____ copy(ies) of ***Corporate Games*** ($27.95 each plus tax, shipping and handling per copy).

Sales Tax (applicable to Shipping address)
Please add 2.9% sales tax for products shipped to Colorado addresses. Within El Paso County, CO, add an additional 1.0% (3.9% total).

Shipping
Continental US: 2-day $12.50 per copy, ground $6.50 per copy.
Alaska and Hawaii: 2-day only, $18.00 per copy.
Canada: ground $9.50 per copy. Call for other international rates.
(Rates subject to change.)

Corporate Games   _____copy(ies) X $27.95   _____

Sales tax if applicable   _____

Shipping (2-day)   _____copy(ies) X $_____   _____

OR Shipping (ground) _____copy(ies) X $_____   _____

TOTAL   _____

Quick Order Form continued on reverse side

www.coolriverpub.com

Name _____

Billing Address _____

City _____ State _____ Zip _____

Shipping Address _____
      (if different from Billing Address)

City _____ State _____ Zip _____

Telephone _____

Email address _____

Payment: Check or
              Credit Card (please circle card used).

   Visa   MasterCard   AMEX   Discover

Card number _____

Name on card _____Exp. Date ___/___

www.coolriverpub.com

Cool River Publishing
Quick Order Form

WEB www.coolriverpub.com
PHONE 719.487.1827 or 800.338.3892   FAX 719.487.1767
POSTAL ORDERS
Cool River Publishing, Alan Hirschfeld
590 Highway 105 #301 • Monument, CO 80132 USA

Please send _____ copy(ies) of **Corporate Games** ($27.95 each plus tax, shipping and handling per copy).

Sales Tax (applicable to Shipping address)
Please add 2.9% sales tax for products shipped to Colorado addresses. Within El Paso County, CO, add an additional 1.0% (3.9% total).

Shipping
Continental US: 2-day $12.50 per copy, ground $6.50 per copy.
Alaska and Hawaii: 2-day only, $18.00 per copy.
Canada: ground $9.50 per copy. Call for other international rates.
(Rates subject to change.)

Corporate Games   _____copy(ies) X $27.95   _____

Sales tax if applicable   _____

Shipping (2-day)   _____copy(ies) X $_____   _____

OR Shipping (ground) _____copy(ies) X $_____   _____

                        TOTAL   _____

Quick Order Form continued on reverse side

www.coolriverpub.com

Name _____

Billing Address _____

City _____ State _____ Zip _____

Shipping Address _____
       (if different from Billing Address)

City _____ State _____ Zip _____

Telephone _____

Email address _____

Payment: Check or
                 Credit Card (please circle card used).

    Visa   MasterCard   AMEX   Discover

Card number _____

Name on card _____Exp. Date ___/___

www.coolriverpub.com